MW01087652

READY FOR KINDERGARTEN?

FREE YOURSELF FROM THE READINESS TRAP SO THAT YOU AND YOUR CHILD ARE READY FOR AND WILL SUCCEED IN KINDERGARTEN

DR. CHRISTOPHER P. BROWN

Published by Advantage Publishing Group

Copyright ©2020, Dr. Christopher P. Brown

Hardcover: ISBN: 978-1-954024-03-8
Paperback: ISBN: 978-1-954024-04-5
eBook: ISBN: 978-1-954024-05-2

https://advantage-publishing.com
To contact, please e-mail: profchrispbro@gmail.com

TABLE OF CONTENTS

INTRODUCTION

Every day, as a parent(s)[i], there's a moment when you look at your child and ask yourself,

- "Am I doing enough?" "Am I feeding her the right food?" "Do we spend enough time together?"
- "Am I giving him enough opportunities in life so that he can figure out who he wants to be?"
- "Am I doing enough to ensure she's ready—be it at school, life, or the next play date with her friends?"

And as a parent, you rarely say, "Yes" to any of these questions. Instead, you worry. Even with all the success you and your child have had together, there's always something to worry about.

This book helps tackle one of these *big* worries, the worry that comes about when you ask yourself this question, "Is my child ready for kindergarten?" (For a quick checklist to see how you're feeling about your child's readiness for school: https://tinyurl.com/cpb-checklist)

The Readiness Trap

You're reading this book because you're nervous about whether or not your child is ready for kindergarten. You're wondering, "Is my child ready?" Or, even possibly, "Am *I* ready to send her/him to kindergarten?" And while you've sought out the advice of family members, friends, or even an educator or administrator, you've come to realize that you now have very different answers to what is actually a simple question.

You're stuck in the *Readiness Trap.* The trap is that first sense of doubt you have as a parent about whether or not your child is ready for kindergarten. Once that doubt enters your mind, you're caught. You find yourself constantly wondering whether or not your child is ready for school. What was once a question you never thought about, now consumes you. This consumption can overtake almost any decision you make about your child and can cause you to doubt yourself and your child.

For example, I once found myself with my wife, Michele, pregnant with our third, and our two daughters waiting for our food at a diner near our home when the mother of two boys in the booth next to us asked the age of our two girls, Camille and Vivienne. At the time, Camille was five and

Vivienne four. Typical parent bantering went on for a while (i.e., how old are your girls, where does Camille go to kindergarten, is Vivienne in preschool, etc.).

When hearing Vivienne was four, the woman asked, "What month was she born in?" Michele answered, "Her birthday was a few weeks ago in October," and the woman commented, "Oh, she has a lucky birthday." Michele and I both looked at each other a little confused because we had never heard of a child having an unlucky birthday. The woman then added, "You know, for kindergarten. She'll be almost six when she starts kindergarten."

Not knowing how to respond when someone tells you that their child has an unlucky birthday (and knowing that our third daughter, Lucille, would arrive in June), we both respectfully said, "Oh, we never thought about that."

The woman continued the conversation by saying, "You know, I've been struggling with whether or not to hold him back. His teacher at his preschool tells us that with summer birthdays, it's a good idea to hold children back, particularly with boys." Since our girls were sitting there with us, we didn't want to raise any alarm about them possibly being held out of kindergarten for an extra year, so Michele and I politely changed the subject until our food was ready.

Michele and I could visibly see, and even physically feel, this mother's guilt over when she gave birth to her son. *No parent* should have to feel this way about her/his child's birthday. Yet, this mother was one of the many I've talked to over the years about the issue of school readiness. She, like all parents, wanted to do everything she could to make sure her child was ready for kindergarten. However, she'd been told her son had an unlucky birthday, and she decided to hold him out of school for an extra year so that he would be older when he entered kindergarten—often called academic redshirting.

This mother's guilt is what ensnares parents in the Readiness Trap. Since the trap feeds off this guilt, it is also built upon a lot of misinformation and misconceptions about early childhood development, the learning processes, and schooling.

No one needs any more guilt in his or her life, particularly about being a good or bad parent. You may not have even known you were supposed to be worried about your child's readiness for school until a friend, caregiver, or relative asked you about it.

If you are anxious about what to do about sending your child to kindergarten when s/he is eligible or are just a parent looking for ideas about how to process as well as manage the notion of making sure your child is ready for kindergarten, you have the right book. This book will help you avoid falling into the trap so you can send your child off to kindergarten with confidence.

If you're like the mother above and are already stuck in the trap, I provide you with a way out. I do so by providing you with information about what is known regarding school readiness. I also prepare you and your child for the current landscape of schooling, including being ready to address common issues that arise during the first year of elementary school.

In helping you set yourself free, *no child* has a lucky or unlucky birthday. The mother in the above was misinformed about the issue of school readiness and academic redshirting, which is how many parents fall into the Readiness Trap.

My Experience with the Readiness Trap

For over two decades, I too have faced issues surrounding this idea of whether or not children are ready for kindergarten both personally and professionally. On a personal level, I've been married for the past 23 years to my wife Michele. We are raising three dynamic, creative, and intelligent young girls: Camille, age 19, Vivienne, age 17, and Lucille, 13. Each child was sent to kindergarten the August following her fifth birthday—Camille turned five in December, Vivienne in October, and Lucille in June.

Michele and I rarely heard any talk of school readiness until the girls got into their later preschool years—ages three and older. When Camille was entering kindergarten, the talk around school readiness seemed less intense, but as Vivienne and then Lucy came of age, my wife stated that she felt that the conversations were becoming more heated. It also appeared that the preschools were becoming more invested in retaining students for one additional year, particularly with Lucille, who would be a "young" kindergartner.

Professionally, I am a Professor of Early Childhood Education at the University of Texas at Austin. I started to study the issue of school readiness at the University of Wisconsin with Dr. M. Elizabeth (Beth) Graue[ii] and have continued to do so[iii] since that time.

I am also a former preschool, kindergarten, and first grade teacher. I have worked with a range of children; as a kindergarten teacher, I even taught a group of 22 kindergarteners, five of whom were born in the month of August. These three boys and two girls were ready for school and had a great kindergarten year.

Because of what I do, I have had many friends, colleagues, and even acquaintances ask me what they should do with their children. The first question I always ask is, "What do you want to do?" In this book, I will walk you through the various issues facing parents of young children. This is the same approach I take with the people I talk to in real life.

> For a free chapter on what to do when your child did not go to preschool click here:
> **https://tinyurl.com/cpb-preschool**

Helping You Move Forward with Your Child

This book will help you become a more informed parent so that you can replace your worry about your child with wisdom. By the time you have completed reading this book, you will know what to do. You can decide whether or not to send your child to kindergarten based on what I share with you in this book and how well you know your child. Once *YOU* decide to send your child to kindergarten, you will do so with confidence. You will be more knowledgeable about the landscape of schooling your child is entering. You will be prepared to address common issues that might arise during the first year of elementary school. (Here's a quick checklist to see how you're feeling about your child's readiness for school: https://tinyurl.com/cpb-checklist)

So **let's get started** so that you can let go of any worry or guilt you may feel about sending your child to kindergarten. The sooner you choose to let go, the sooner you can go back to the joy of parenting while knowing that you've made the right decision.

CHAPTER 1

Defining What it Means for Your Child to be Ready for Kindergarten

Every day, children ask their parents and caregivers to define or explain something—e.g., "What does 'fascinating' mean?" Or, "Why can birds fly and I can't?" However, when it comes to the issue of school readiness, defining it can be very complex. Not only have the expectations for what children need to learn in kindergarten changed over the years,[iv] but research has shown that how one community thinks about school readiness can be very different from another.[v]

Making Sense of School Readiness

How policymakers, educators, and families make sense of school readiness varies depending on the issue being discussed and the context in which they live and work.[vi] As Beth Graue noted long ago, "Readiness is the answer to many different kinds of questions." [vii] The easiest way to make sense of the complexity surrounding school readiness is by framing it as a basic equation--the sum of the equation being the ready child.[viii] The variables within the equation reflect policymakers' reforms, society's values, your own values and what is known about child development and learning.

How each variable is defined as well as weighted within the equation affects not only how school personnel view your child's readiness but also how you think about school readiness. For example, when thinking about education reform and school readiness, policymakers are addressing this issue by putting in place particular policies. These policies are there to address specific variables within the readiness equation.

To be able to interpret these different types of equations, Dr. Samuel Meisels,[ix] a researcher who has studied the issue of school readiness since the 1980s, outlines four conceptions of school readiness. These concepts capture the ways in which researchers, policymakers, and early education advocates typically frame the school readiness equation: an idealist, empiricist, social constructionist, and interactionist conception of school readiness.

Defining Meisels' four conceptions of school readiness

An **idealist** frames readiness as a function of the child, meaning readiness is dependent on the child's development. If you know anything about child development, think Piaget's ages and stages. An idealist thinks there is an internal clock in the child based on her/his "maturational processes" that determines whether s/he is ready for school.[x]

An **empiricist** views "readiness [as] something that lies outside the child."[xi] As such, an empiricist believes that the child needs to engage in a specific set of experiences to be ready for school.

A **social constructionist** views school readiness as a fluid construct that is defined by the social setting in which the child resides—culture and context play a significant role in this understanding of school readiness. So how school readiness is defined is dependent on the context in which the child lives (e.g., living in Dallas, TX or Boise, ID), which means a child can be viewed as being ready for school in one community but not another.[xii]

An **interactionist** frames readiness as a "bidirectional concept," which means readiness is co-constructed "from the child's contributions to schooling and the school's contribution to the child."[xiii] This lens recognizes that school readiness is a contribution of both the home and the school. Thus, it is the responsibility of school personnel to first recognize that all children come to school with different strengths and growth areas.[xiv] Then, they must work with the children and their families to ensure everyone is successful in school.

Why are there so many conceptions of school readiness?

These four conceptions of school readiness illuminate the ways in which policymakers, educators, and families, including you and me, understand the role of the family, teacher, school system, and larger society in preparing children for school success. For instance, when parents ask whether their child is old enough for kindergarten, that frames school readiness through an idealist perspective—age is the determining factor. When parents ask what their child needs to know or what they should have experienced (e.g., preschool) to be ready for kindergarten, that reflects an empiricist understanding of school readiness—having certain learning experiences, knowledge and skills determines whether a child is ready. Parents who have friends and family who live in different communities and are told very different things about what it means to be ready for school (e.g., a sister telling them a child needs to be able to count to 20 versus a neighbor saying children only need to count to 10 in the local school). This exemplifies a social constructivist framing of this construct. Lastly, when parents ask how they can help their child's teacher see the strengths their child brings to the classroom, they are seeing school readiness as an interaction, or what Meisels terms the interactionist perspective.

In the current context of schooling, policymakers' reforms focus on readying children for school, which takes an empiricist perspective—providing children with an early childhood education (ECE) program, such as pre-kindergarten, or an intervention to readying them for school (see the equation below).

An empiricist conception of school readiness

Early childhood advocates and organizations such as NAEYC, the National Association for the Education of Young Children (the largest professional organization for early childhood educators in the US), promote an interactionist view of school readiness. This view considers the role of the child, family, teacher, school, and the community-at-large (see the equation below).[xv]

An interactionist conception of school readiness

While policymakers and early education stakeholders often think about school readiness in different ways, what matters is whether or not your child will be seen as being ready for kindergarten by her/his teachers, classmates, and other school personnel. Those skills, traits, and notions of readiness have evolved in recent years because kindergarten has changed so much.[xvi] It is often referred to "the new first grade"[xvii]--I call it the "changed kindergarten" or the "Kinder-Race"[xviii] because children are expected to race from learning one skill to the next.

The Changed Kindergarten/Kinder-Race

Kindergarten today is no longer seen as an introduction for children into how school works, including how to function in a school community.[xix] Rather, it is a learning environment in which teachers must meet "prescribed curricular mandates and uniform standards." They have to teach children "advanced academic content" through "teacher-directed whole group instruction" as well as prepare them for "much more standardized testing."[xx] This change reflects policymakers at all levels of governance continued focus on improving children's academic achievement through the use of standardized instructional practices. They promote such policies so that all students can obtain a specific set of knowledge and skills by the time they leave secondary school.[xxi]

Examples of these changes have been documented by researchers such as Daphna Bassok and her colleagues at the University of Virginia. They analyzed data from two kindergarten cohorts that participated in the Early Childhood Longitudinal Study (ECLS-K:1998 and ECLS-K:2011).[xxii] From the 1998 school year to the 2010 school year, they found a large increase in the time kindergarten teachers spent on academic skills instruction as well as giving children more standardized assessments while spending less time on child-selected activities (playing in the block center), music, and art.

Another set of researchers, Alford, Rollins, Padrón, and Waxman, studied a total of 91 classrooms across 21 elementary schools, including pre-kindergarten (Pre-K), kindergarten, first grade, and second grade classrooms, in a large south-central city in the US. They found that no matter the grade level, these teachers "consistently utilized whole class, didactic, teacher-centered instructional practices in their classrooms—regardless of the sex and/or ethnic make-up of their students."[xxiii]

Lastly, I have been researching how education stakeholders from the classroom to the statehouse make sense of the changed kindergarten.[xxiv.] To put it simply, most people are uncomfortable with kindergarten being the "new" first grade. They do not like seeing children and teachers working in a school environment where the children are expected to race from learning one skill to the next.

Why these changes matter. The intensification around the issues of school readiness and the changed kindergarten is significant because what happens in kindergarten seems to affect children's success in and out of school.[xxv] Researchers have found that readiness for kindergarten influences the types of relationships children are able to establish with their peers and their teachers.[xxvi] It also affects their ability to attend to academic learning experiences[xxvii] and can impact their trajectory of academic performance as they progress through school and into adulthood.[xxviii]

To put it bluntly, if children enter kindergarten at age five significantly lagging behind their peers in cognitive and social measures, it is less likely they will be successful in grade school. They will also be more likely to drop out of high school and are projected to earn less as adults.[xxix] Additionally, these gaps in children's academic and social achievement, which can be found across the globe,[xxx] can increase across their time in school.[xxxi]

I know all of that sounds scary, but let me clarify what these researchers mean when they are discussing children's readiness for kindergarten. One of the key data sources for these studies comes out of the Early Childhood Longitudinal Study (https://nces.ed.gov/ecls/instruments2011.asp); this study has been going on since 1998. This longitudinal study follows three different cohorts of children from across the US as they progress through school. The birth cohort of the ECLS-B follows children born in 2001 from birth through kindergarten; the 1998-99 kindergarten cohort follows children from kindergarten through the eighth grade; the 2010-11 kindergarten cohort is following a sample of children from kindergarten through the fifth grade. This study uses reports from teachers and parents to measure the child's academic and social skills when entering kindergarten. For the 2010-11 kindergarten cohort study, the teacher is asked to evaluate the child's academic skill level through a series of 25 questions (see page 4 of https://nces.ed.gov/ecls/pdf/kinder-garten2011/Fall_K_Classroom_Teacher_Child_Level.pdf).

The teacher is asked whether the child can sort, classify, and compare math materials by various rules and attributes. For example, does the child understand the relationship between quantities? Does the child understand that a group of ten small stones is the same quantity as a group of ten larger blocks? The teacher could also be asked to rate the child on her/his skill using a continuum of performance that ranges from not possessing the skill to being proficient.

If you look at these 25 items, they are not complex skills (e.g. the child understands and interprets a story or other text read to him/her); therefore, the child should either be developing or possess these skills by the end of kindergarten. Essentially, any child who has had some experience with counting, comparing, and measuring, will do fine on these assessments.

Unfortunately, there are many children who enter school without being given either the vocabulary to demonstrate what they know about mathematics or having the opportunity to experiment with such mathematical knowledge either with a more knowledgeable peer or adult. *This is not your child*, but you need to know that much the empirical work that explores these issues is simply trying to find correlations between skills and school readiness. This is significant because it helps early educators think about what they should focus on in their curricula and instruction.

These researchers are not thinking about whether or not to send a child to kindergarten. My own research[xxxii] has shown that *ALL* families in the US, no matter their education level, income status, or cultural background, want their children to succeed in school. So, yes, where a child is academically and socially when s/he enters kindergarten matters; however, a child's future in school and/or life cannot be predicted at age

5. There have been a range of studies that contradict the idea that children's level of academic and social performance is fixed at kindergarten.[xxxiii] Most importantly, your child has more than likely been exposed to and/or already knows many of the skills that these studies measure.

If you're still worried, do not worry. By the end of this book, you will not be. Instead, you'll be confident in your decision about sending your child to kindergarten.

Families and Teachers' Understanding of School Readiness

As kindergarten has changed, so have families and teachers' conceptions of what it means for children to be ready for kindergarten. Generally speaking, families typically frame what it means for children to be ready for school through a range of academic skills such as counting, reading, and writing.[xxxiv]

Still,[xxxv] there are some common trends in studies that match how you might be feeling toward your child's readiness for school. For example, researchers have consistently found that families typically have some doubt about their child's readiness for school. A study conducted by Hatcher and her colleagues dove into how teachers and families thought about school readiness. For example, a parent in the study stated, "I'm just afraid of the whole reading thing...I'm hoping the whole reading and stuff won't overwhelm her when she gets there…I'm thinking she's ready. I'm just still afraid of the reading."[xxxvi] Even though most parents are worried, no matter their sociocultural background or economic status,[xxxvii] they want their children to succeed in school and are willing to do whatever it takes to make that happen.

Teachers are more likely to define school readiness in terms that extend beyond children's academic skills.[xxxviii] For instance, some researchers have used their findings to contend that teachers prioritize children's non-academic skills. For example, children's attitudes towards school and their ability to work independently.[xxxix] However, recent work with my colleague[xl] found that teachers' conceptions about school readiness have focused more on academics since the implementation of the *No Child Left Behind Act* (NCLB) in 2002. This means what occurs in kindergarten matters for children. Also, what has been occurring over the last two decades is a focus by all stakeholders to ensure children gain the academic skills and knowledge they need to succeed in school.

How School Readiness is Often Defined

The definition of school readiness has not only changed in recent years, but how it is defined also depends on where you live and the school you plan to send your child to for kindergarten. Most public kindergarten programs have some form of open house in the spring or early summer to help parents register and learn about kindergarten. In Texas, they are often called kindergarten round-ups. They are designed to register new families in the district, inform them about what kindergarten is all about, and to let the children see where they will be going to school the next year.

When I taught kindergarten, during the open house, the other kindergarten teachers and I would have the children play in the kindergarten classrooms without their families. Some of the teachers in the room took notes on which children appeared to handle the transition easily and worked well with others. We would also schedule one-on-one appointments with families in the spring so that could bring their child in to work with the teachers on a couple of fun activities. This is done so the teachers could get a sense of whether the children knew such things as how to follow directions, cut, glue, write their name, and identify some basic numbers and letters. We used this information to place students into their future classrooms. We tried to ensure that there was a balance in both social and academic skills among the classrooms. We would then assess the children again once they entered kindergarten to make sure we were teaching to each child's level.

Kindergarten teachers, myself included, want children to be able to follow directions, get along with their peers, and have some basic academic skills. If you were to google "kindergarten readiness checklists" you would see both "free" and for purchase checklists.

One that I likes comes from the American Federation of Teachers (https://tinyurl.com/aftreadiness-checklist) and another from a group called Understood, which is a collection of 15 nonprofit organizations who work together to support parents of children with learning and attention issues (https://tinyurl.com/understoodpdf). Both sets of checklists try to capture a holistic vision of your child as a learner. You should not expect your child to be able to do all these things before s/he enters kindergarten (I talk more about this in the following paragraphs, so please do not start assessing your child after reading the examples below).

Some of the skills they assess on these checklists include:

- Can your child use a pencil, scissors, run, jump, skip, and hop?
- Can your child use the bathroom and wash themselves independently?
- Can s/he count to 10, match a group of 5 to the number, understands more or less?
- Can s/he write her/his own name?
- Does s/he recognize when two words rhyme?
- Can s/he recite the alphabet?
- Does s/he know most of the letters (capital and lowercase)?
- Can s/he begin to identify letters with their sounds (e.g., the sound the letter 't' makes)?

- Can your child concentrate on a task?
- Can s/he remember nursery rhymes easily?
- Can your child follow directions?
- Does your child respond appropriately to other adults?
- Does s/he show interests in other children?
- Can s/he pay attention for 5 minutes to a task an adult is leading?

I *DO NOT* want you to think about this list of skills as an absolute or perfect measure of school readiness. Remember, think about school readiness as an equation. What your child contributes to that equation is going to vary based on who s/he is as an individual. Moreover, depending on when in your child's life you're reading this book (e.g., your child is only 3), your daughter or son is going to change significantly between now and when s/he enters kindergarten, and s/he'll change even more once in kindergarten.

So please *DO NOT* obsess over these lists or buy books and start testing your child; do not use them as a series of lessons you need to teach your child either. That's not my intent in sharing them with you. Rather, they are simply a guide for you to think about how others define the skills and traits associated with school readiness. Your child should be developing these academic skills as s/he turns five. If you want to help them develop these skills, you should do so in a natural and/or fun way (e.g., pointing out individual letters when reading a book or counting the number of napkins needed for dinner with the family). Moreover, when looking at these or any "list," you should understand that the skills kindergarten teachers most often want your child to have at the beginning of the school year are social (e.g., paying attention for five minutes on a task an adult is leading) and self-care skills (e.g., using the bathroom and washing themselves independently).

When looking at these lists and thinking about them holistically, they cover what Kagan and her colleagues[xli] identified as the five dimensions of school readiness: a) physical well-being and development, b) social and emotional development, c) approaches to learning, d) language development, and e) cognition and general development. Still, when looking at these five dimensions and the lists I cited above, they measure *easily observable skills*, and in doing so, they leave out a lot. For example, they do not address issues of sex, birthdays, or the importance of you and your child's sociocultural contexts all of which shapes the way your child develops and learns.

These omissions *are significant* when thinking about the school readiness equation for multiple reasons. First, in terms of sex, boys are often framed as being more immature than girls. In many instances, family members project their own sports aspirations on to their children, particularly boys, as they think about entering kindergarten. For example, I live in

Texas, and if you've ever heard of the saying "Friday Night Lights," which was made popular by a book, movie, and TV series, you would know how important high school football is to many Texans. As such, many parents who have boys think about how old their child will be when he enters high school. They know that if he is a year older he should be taller and a bit heavier; with football, size does matter. No checklist I've ever seen asks whether or not you want your son to play high school football.

Also, when a child is born appears to play a large role in how readiness is discussed—there's an assumption that age determines development, which is an inaccurate understanding of children's learning and development. Age can mark a developmental range as to where a child typically should 'be' in relation to both physical characteristics and developmental skills; however, research has consistently shown that Piaget's notion of ages and stages is *incorrect*.[xlii]

Rather, I, and many of my colleagues,[xliii] want you to recognize that, according to Vygotsky,[xliv] *learning leads development*; it's a social process where interactions with peers, adults, or teachers assists children in developing the skills and knowledge needed to make sense of and operate in the larger world. Meaning, if a child has been read to since s/he was born, s/he is not only learning the structure of language, the written word, and story-telling, but s/he will be primed to learn such literacy skills as identifying the part of a book (e.g., cover, title, author, illustrator, etc.) from her/his teacher compared to a child who has had very limited experience with formal texts.

These checklists also assume all children come from the same backgrounds, which is a big omission in thinking about learning, development, and schooling. Various cultures view the role of the child and the learning process differently, which can affect how the child views the world and approaches new problems. It also has a significant impact on her/his long-term memory, which shapes how s/he thinks about and interacts with learning in the here and now. Moreover, what occurs in the home environment also impacts children's development and learning in significant ways. For instance, children who come from high-stress home environments or from homes where the caregivers are emotionally unavailable to them often show delays in their cognitive functioning,[xlv] again, this is not you or your child.

So while developmental theory and psychology makes it appear as if there is a natural course to human development,[xlvi] *there is not.* When thinking about school readiness you as well as the school personnel you will work with should not focus on what's easiest to measure (e.g., can your child write her/his name). Rather, you should first think about the sociocultural world in which you are raising your child. Think about what is most valuable to you and your family when preparing your child for the larger world.

With this in mind, think about how your values/beliefs stack up against these easily identifiable skills and traits. From there, how might you be able to prepare your child and her/his future kindergarten teacher for what you see your child being- -a ready child! By doing this, you can begin to develop an interactionist relationship with your child's teacher and school.

Is Your Child Ready for Kindergarten?

Do *you* think your child is ready? This may not be an easy question to answer, and honestly, it's a bit unfair for me to put that on you so early into this book. However, the ideas behind these checklists, tutoring companies, etc, make it seem like if you do x, y, or z, your child will be ready for kindergarten.

Such logic ignores all the other factors that influence how the readiness of your child will be viewed by yourself and by others. In the next chapter, I explore why school readiness has become such a big deal, and this will help you understand why you feel so anxious when someone asks you, "Is your child ready for kindergarten?"

Key Points to Remember

There are 4 common ways people frame school readiness:

1) An idealist sees readiness in the child; so a child is ready for kindergarten when s/he turns 5.

2) An empiricist sees readiness outside the child; so a child can be readied for school by having certain experiences.

3) A social constructionist views school readiness as being dependent on context—so what school readiness looks like in New York City is probably different from El Paso, TX.

4) An interactionist frames readiness as a multidimensional construct that considers the child, the community s/he lives in, her/his family, the school, and so on.

- Kindergarten has become academic in recent years, meaning teachers spend more time on teaching academic content than preparing children for how the school system works.

- How families and teachers define what it means for a child to be ready for school may differ but both want all children to succeed in school.

- There are checklists that provide insight into common traits that children should possess when going into kindergarten, but these are general guidelines that should be seen as tools to help you make more informed decisions about your child's growth and development--STILL, all of this can make you uncomfortable but don't let it. You know your child, and by the end of this book, you will be confident in the decision you will make about sending her/him to school.

- Lastly, learning leads development; learning is a social process where interactions with peers, adults, or teachers assists children into developing the skills and knowledge they need in order to make sense of and operate in the larger world, including kindergarten.

CHAPTER 2

Why Your Child's Readiness for School is Such a Big Deal: School Readiness as a Social Issue

One Saturday afternoon, Michele and I were sitting around our kitchen table with Lucille, Vivienne, and Vivienne's friend Kendall,[xlvii] eating nachos. They were talking about birthdays and what month each of them were born in. In turns out, both Kendall and Lucy were born in June. Kendall asked Lucy what grade she was in, which at the time was kindergarten. Kendall said, "Oh, okay, if you were a boy, your parents probably would have held you back." Michele and I looked at each other, and Michele politely asked, "What do you mean?"

Kendall continued, "Because I am a girl, my parents decided to send me to kindergarten when I was five, but with my older brother, who was also born in June, my parents decided to hold him back so that he can be bigger for football in high school." Michele and I both said "Okay," and Kendall continued. "You know, that's what parents do with boys. They want them to be bigger in high school so that they can be on the football team." Michele and I both nodded our heads and the conversation among the girls continued.

It is amazing that children, including my own, are aware of the issue of school readiness. In fact, they know it as soon as they enter school. When my youngest, Lucille, was in kindergarten, there were children, mostly boys, but not all, who were a year older than she was. This trend was seen in my older girls' kindergarten classes too. When each of them first became aware that they had classmates a year older than they were, they asked us if something was wrong with the older kids. Each thought that those children had been held back because they failed kindergarten, which made them worry that they might fail kindergarten too. I had to explain the idea of academic redshirting to each of them. This simply means parents decide to hold their child out of kindergarten/elementary school for an extra year even though their child meets the age requirement. After I explained this, they of course asked, "Why didn't you hold us back?" That's when I go off an academic diatribe, but then, Michele shakes her head at me and simply says to whichever girl asked, "We sent you to kindergarten because you were ready."

Both of these anecdotes reveal the pervasiveness of this issue of school readiness. As parents, we are not immune to these pressures about whether our children are ready for kindergarten, even if our children know something is up that doesn't quite make sense. In this chapter, I examine one of the two primary "forces" that make school readiness such a big deal: school readiness as a social issue. In the next chapter, I examine school readiness as a policy issue.

For you and for most families, the issue of school readiness is primarily a personal/social issue; you may be worried about whether your child is ready to perform as soon as s/he walks in the kindergarten door. You might feel as if s/he is not ready or you might think s/he will never catch up. Or you may be like Kendall's family, you want to ensure your child makes the varsity team of whatever sport you're interested in when s/he is in high school. Other concerns parents have about sending their child to kindergarten include what grade their child will be in when s/he can legally drive a car, how old s/he'll be when s/he enters college or turns 21.[xlviii]

TMI (Too Much Information)

The input of friends, family members, and popular media might also add pressure to an already confusing situation. In fact, the issue of school readiness typically does not come up for many families until they either talk with their child's preschool teacher, a friend or family member who has an older child, or open a magazine/newspaper and see an article on starting kindergarten on time or redshirting your child. In some cases, preschools and/or local elementary schools have school readiness seminars where they talk about what it means for a child to be ready for school. All of these examples demonstrate how we live in a world where we are inundated with so much information that it's easy to become misinformed about these things we truly care about, including the readiness of your child to enter kindergarten.

To put it bluntly, most families worry more than they need to over the question of whether or not their child is ready for kindergarten. It is this increased worrying over school readiness that has led to the creation of new markets for products and services that not only feed off the school Readiness Trap but also intensify it. For instance, there are now school readiness camps in the summer for four and five year-old children that are supposed to give them a head start for kindergarten or first grade entry. There are companies that offer tutoring services to children as young as age three to help them improve their child's academic skills—typically in reading or in mathematics. Families even buy the readiness tests I referred to in the last chapter to see if their child is ready for kindergarten. And of course, every parent knows about the "educational" toys, videos, songs, and so on that claim to give a child an extra boost for school success. All of these products and services perpetuate the idea that whatever it is they have to offer will somehow provide your child with a leg up on the "competition," which may even be your child's best friend.

From a research perspective, claims by many marketers that their products are research based and will ready your child for school are misleading at best. Much of the research these companies use to verify the effectiveness of their products was not conducted with young children. The most famous of these ideas being the Mozart effect: exposure to classical music will improve your child's brain development. This effect came from research done with college students on a standardized assessment[xlix]—this has nothing to do with having your child listen to classical music, which can be soothing as well as providing the child with a different type of listening experience. Disney had to pay a hefty piece when it came to light that the products of the Little Einstein Company it purchased did not yield baby geniuses.[l]

"What" is at stake?

When thinking about school readiness as a policy problem, it's easy to think about school readiness as an issue of student achievement and/or a nation's economic/academic competitiveness. Doing so frames the solution to the problem as simply requiring more of something: more financial support for children and their families to help them gain access to preschool, or more early childhood training for preschool and kindergarten teachers to improve their students' academic performance.

When thinking about school readiness as a social issue, defining the problem as well as its solution becomes much trickier. Still, much of this social concern over school readiness can be boiled down to two issues: 1) competitive advantage for your child, 2) competitive advantage for your child's teacher.

Competitive advantage for your child

In terms of competitive advantage for your child, there is an underlying belief within the social world that a person's trajectory for success in life (both personally and economically) can be set at an early age. While there is some research that supports this claim, there are other studies that debunk it. Most often, a child's success is determined by the wealth of the family s/he is born into and the education level of her parents.[li]

Nevertheless, research has shown that at best, there is a boost for children being older in the early grades that flattens out as they progress through school. For example, the work of Bedard and Dhuey[lii], which Elizabeth Weil[liii] and Malcolm Gladwell[liv] made famous over a decade ago, shows a positive correlation to being an older rather than younger child at grade entry on academic measures in grades 4 and 8 and a greater likelihood that s/he will take the SAT and ACT. But, Bedard and Dhuey also found no correlation between the age a child enters school and how long that child attends school—which correlates with college completion and graduate school attendance.

Furthermore, other researchers, such as Black, Devereux, and Salvanes,[lv] have found starting older has no effect on intelligence or school performance; in fact, it can negatively affect an individual's overall lifetime earnings. In some instances, researchers have shown a benefit to being younger in school. For instance, Morrison, Griffith, and Alberts[lvi] found that younger first grade children in Canada made as much progress in reading and math as their older peers and much more progress than older kindergarteners, which would be similar in age. Cascio and Schanzenbach[lvii] who studied kindergarteners in Tennessee, also found children who were young relative to their kindergarten classmates generally performed no worse on achievement tests, were no more likely to be retained, and were no less likely to take the ACT or SAT. In fact, they found having older classmates on average improves students' educational outcomes, increasing test scores up to eight years after kindergarten.

While that's a lot of information at once, what these researchers are often trying to figure out is what Bedard and Dhuey refer to as the multiplier effect or Gladwell calls the "Matthew effect,"[lviii] where skill acquisition leads to further development for the child. This means that the skills gained in the early years help create a foundation upon which later skills are developed. So those children who develop a range of developmental skills early on benefit from the continued growth and development of these skills as they proceed through school, which is why the wealth of the family you're born into matters—more money usually means access to more resources and experiences.

A birthday is not a death sentence. No matter which you believe in, it is quite alarming when a parent/family, teacher, or school administrator assumes a child's life trajectory is set by a certain age. Can you imagine assuming your life was "set" for you by the age of 3, 5, 9, or even 20? In essence, you're stating that human development is static and fixed, which it's not.[lix] Also, it means that you are denying your impact as a parent, as well the impact of your family, community, and schools on your child's development.

When looking at what impacts children's lives from a statistical standpoint and what might predict their success, there are all sorts of indicators that have been correlated to your child's development (e.g., consistently having access to food, clothing, and shelter, being a part of a two parent family, a mother's level of education, and/or divorced parents). And of course, there are counter studies that raise questions about how closely correlated these indicators actually are to a child's development.

No matter what you decide about enrolling your child in kindergarten, there are millions of other factors, interactions, and choices that you and your child will make that will have either a positive and/or negative impact on your child's development and/or success in school. Remember, you can only control so much, and for everything else, you have to be willing to accept what happens, correct what you can and/or admit your mistakes, and move on. "WE" are a resilient species, and WE need to remember "that" as WE love and support our children through their growth and development.

Keep reading. You are reading this book because you are seeking out ways to make an informed decision as well as provide opportunities to your child that can improve her/his likelihood to lead a successful life. Trying to activate such competitive advantages permeates such issues as the school(s) you will send your child to, the activities you will enroll them in, and the community you will raise your child in.

All of these issues focus on you, your partner, and your child. What concerns me about this idea of competitive advantage is that "WE", as in "WE" the people in the United States, have become much more individualistic. "WE" as a society have either lost faith in, or for some reason, associated community-based and/or government support with weakness or inefficiency. I bring up this issue because it affects the way I think about school readiness and the Readiness Trap.

By focusing on the competitive advantage of your child, it appears to put the locus of control over your child's life in your hands, and as such, any sort of success or failure is the result of your actions. This washes away any responsibility for the system/society in which you live (i.e., the schools your child attends, the quality of the air you breath/water you drink/food you eat, or access to medical care). So, if you don't have access to high-quality preschool, health care, or water, it's your fault. The "assumption" is that you can always move, find a better job, or make some other choice. In bringing this issue up, I also know how difficult it is to be a parent. I recognize how much pressure you feel to be a great, let alone, good parent. I applaud your efforts.

This issue of meeting the needs of your individual child versus supporting the collective whole ties directly to such issues as the quality of the public schools your child will (or will not) attend. This is influenced by the quality of teacher who works there, the shape the school building is in, and what the teacher and school are expected to teach. When thinking about the issues of school readiness or the Readiness Trap and possible ways to avoid falling into it, it is helpful to think about solutions that not only benefit you and your child but also society at large, including the schools your child will attend. Moreover, by simply focusing on the needs and success of your child, it lets teachers, school administrators, and policymakers off the hook. Thinking back to the interactionist readiness equation,[lx] teachers/schools need to be ready for any children who come into their classroom. While I want to help you help your child succeed in school, I also want to ensure every child has a chance to succeed in school.

Competitive advantage for the child's teacher

In terms of competitive advantage for the child's teacher, there are two "factors" involved in this issue of school readiness.

The first factor. If your child is enrolled in a privately-run preschool/child care program, older children are where these programs make their money. State licensing regulations as well as accreditation from national organizations such as the NAEYC have specific child-to-teacher ratios in place for each age group of children--the younger the child, the smaller the child-to-teacher ratio needs to be (e.g., one teacher to every four children ages 0 to 18 months). With four- and five-year-olds, programs can have more children under the supervision of one teacher (up to 20 or 22 children). For these private/non-profit programs to survive, they need older children because it deflects the cost of providing more teachers to fewer children in the early years programs; additionally, many states have or are considering expanding access to publicly funded pre-kindergarten (pre-k) programs for three and four year-olds. Taking three, four, or five-year olds out the pool of potential customers/clients can devastate these programs.

Because these programs are so dependent on older children, having them stay an extra year can help their bottom line. To be clear, *I am not saying* this is the reason why a preschool would recommend your child stay an extra year in their program. Yet, I've found in the different communities and neighborhoods in which I've lived that there are programs that make this recommendation more often than others. This is true particularly with boys, which ends up costing the family an additional year of preschool tuition.

There are also programs that start talking about academically redshirting children when they are as young as two years old, again, particularly boys with summer birthdays. Such a recommendation violates everything "we" know about how children learn and develop, which is uneven, can occur in spurts, can be spurred on by direct interaction with a peer or adult, and progress in one developmental domain (social, emotional, cognitive, physical) is dependent upon as well as influences the others.lxii" Such a recommendation also goes against the practices advocated by organizations such as NAEYC, and I want you to be aware of this.

The second factor. The other factor involved in this issue of competitive advantage is the kindergarten teacher and her/his elementary school colleagues, who work in a school environment where policymakers have defined his success by how well the students in her/his classroom achieve academically. This pressure to perform can be seen through the experiences of a friend of Michele at a kindergarten information session.

A friend of Michele, Margaret, went to a kindergarten information session for her daughter who has a summer birthday. The public school was located in an affluent neighborhood that has a reputation for doing well on Texas's high-stakes assessments. The principal and school counselor were there to discuss both the required paperwork to register for kindergarten as well as what to expect for the upcoming school year. The principal kindly informed the families that the kindergarten of today might be very different from the one they remember. She mentioned that there is a greater focus on academic skills development, and as parents, they'll be surprised by how much their children will learn during their first year of school.

During the question and answer period of the session, Margaret said that another mother brought up whether or not she should send her son, who has a summer birthday, to kindergarten. She said the school counselor was quite clear and direct that she felt providing an extra year of preschool for boys with summer birthdays was the appropriate decision to make. She did not give the mother any other information about the complexity of this choice or provide her with any reasons as to why she might want to send her son to kindergarten.

At the end of the session, Margaret went up to the counselor and told her about her daughter and her summer birthday. She told the counselor she was planning to send her, and from what she just told the other mom, it sounded like she was saying that her daughter would automatically be at a disadvantage in her kindergarten classroom if she sent her. The counselor plainly said to our friend that yes, her daughter would be at a disadvantage to older and more mature kindergartners. She then turned to another parent.

The focus on academic achievement in kindergarten has shifted the debate over what it means for any child to be ready for school. In this example, the school counselor associated the age of Margaret's child with whether or not she would be ready to succeed in kindergarten both academically and socially. This is a common misconception (even among school teachers and counselors) when it comes to how children learn and develop the skills needed for school success.

Kindergarten and elementary school teachers have often framed what it means to be ready for school differently than families—emphasizing children's social and emotional skills as well as such non-academic skills as children's attitudes towards school and their ability to work independently rather than academics.[lxi] However, as policymakers have sharpened their focus on academic outcomes,[lxii] empirical research is beginning to document a shift in which teachers tend to prioritize children's academic skills more.[lxiii] This is not to say teachers have abandoned their concerns over a child's level of social development, but rather, a child's academic ability is becoming their primary focus. This means that teachers want children to come to school with both strong academic and social skills. Children who are unable to do this not only affect the dynamics of what takes place in their classroom but also their status as a teacher.

If you combine your concerns about your child's readiness plus your child's teacher's concerns over their own success and the success of their program(s), this creates a highly charged situation. It is important to recognize this because how your child's kindergarten teacher views your child's readiness for school matters since it can affect the types of relationships your child's teacher establishes with her/him. Children who are seen as ready by their kindergarten teacher are more likely to develop positive and close relationships with their teachers, which in turn correlates with improved academic and social-emotional outcomes and long-terms school adjustment.[lxiv] Additionally, establishing a positive relationship between teachers and students correlates with increased academic performance in kindergarten and beyond.[lxv] Thus, competitive advantage affects both you and your child's kindergarten teacher. Even if your child's kindergarten teacher is under a lot of pressure, *do not* let that teacher define your child simply based on your child's sex or birthday.

Popular Media and School Readiness

You are reading this book because you want your child to succeed and because someone or something has caused you to question whether your child is in fact ready for school. Unfortunately, the popular media tends to inflame the "conversation" over whether or not children are ready for school rather than help ease the situation.

It seems as if every spring/summer, right before school starts, an article appears in such news outlets both locally and nationally that discuss the dilemma of whether or not parents should send their 5-year-olds to kindergarten. While these articles typically try to discuss the pros and cons of redshirting your child, they ultimately add to the gravity of your final choice.

So why do these articles re-emerge every year? You would think it is the cyclical nature of kindergarten enrollment, but in many instances, and this has happened to me (as well as to my colleagues), the reporter is interested in this topic because s/he has a young child. Most likely, a boy born in the summer, who has turned five and is struggling with whether or not to send her/his child to school. Little do they know how their initial curiosity amplifies the concerns of their readers.

Another type of article that is often seen almost annually in large city papers during the winter, such as the *New York Times*, is the application process for elite preschool programs.

I mention these articles because families do wonder if the age of their child, which they tie directly to their child's level of maturity, will improve their child's chances of getting in the elite preschool. Combined, these articles will fuel your focus on this issue of competitive advantage.

On a side note, after years of the same old story, media outlets are beginning to investigate alternative programs across the US that have a different view on child learning and development and instruction. Some of these pieces look at play-based kindergarten, outdoor schools, or family run co-ops. These alternative programs emerge either because parents are fed up with the harried nature of the whole process to get one's child accepted to an elite program. Or maybe, the parents/early educators question the current focus of framing school readiness solely on a child's ability to achieve in the here and now; the here and now being a 2 or 3 year-old child.

Moreover, there is an increasing number of articles challenging the push for increased academics in the early years of schooling[lxvi] as well as organizations[lxvii] that raise similar questions. There are also a growing number of pieces written by folks who are taking a more nuanced look at the research that is out there and really thinking about what the research is showing in relation to redshirting or sending kids to kindergarten.[lxviii] It appears the issue of school readiness is being rethought in many different ways.

Time to Reflect

There is no universal principle that determines whether a child is ready for kindergarten. The determining factor is YOU and how you and your family will support your child throughout this process. Still, by being aware of all these competing factors, you should now have a better idea of where you are at in deciding to send your child to kindergarten. If not, that's okay. Either way, I think it's time to put down some thoughts to paper and think about how you are "framing" your child's readiness for kindergarten (if you haven't already done so). Some of these questions are easy to answer. Others are quite difficult. For now, simply identify what's going through your head about this issue so that you can have a clearer sense of what it is you want to know to help you make an informed decision about your child's readiness for kindergarten.

- Where did this idea that my child may not be ready for kindergarten come from?
- How am I defining school readiness?
- How are my friends and/or child's preschool teachers defining school readiness?
- Why do I think my child is not ready for kindergarten? Is it her/his physical size, social skills, motor skills, academic skills, issues of self-control, my concerns over when s/he will drive? Being on the varsity high school sports team?

- How am I supporting my child's growth and development now and as s/he gets closer to being able to enroll in kindergarten?
- Am I going to be able to send her/him to kindergarten without regrets? If not, what are these regrets and why do I think I have them?

As you move through the rest of the book, answering each of these questions will get easier. For now, just be aware of where you are in this decision-making process; by doing so, it will help you retain what you need to know as you read through the rest of the book so that you will make *YOUR* decision with confidence.

Key Points to Remember

Socially, concerns over school readiness boils down to two issues:
  1) Competitive advantage for your child
  2) Competitive advantage for your child's teacher

- It's not when your child was born that will determine her/his success in school. It's the opportunities s/he has and the strength of the community s/he grows up in—so try to think about school readiness as an issue involving not just your child but also you, "where" you live, and the larger world— "we" all need to support the growth and development of every child.

- Because public school teachers are under much more pressure to ensure their students are performing at high academic levels, they often make rash decisions about children's readiness for school based on such issues as gender or birthday—don't let your child's kindergarten teacher define your child that way.

- Take a moment to reflect and put your ideas on paper. Think about where you are at in relation to your decision about sending your child to kindergarten. (See the section titled: Time to Reflect and See Where You are at in your Decision-Making Process to help you think through this issue.)

CHAPTER 3

School Readiness as a Policy Issue

A friend of ours was at her daughter's elementary school with her preschool son in tow to drop off a forgotten lunch. As they were walking to her daughter's classroom, a kindergarten teacher she barely knew stopped her to say hello. Her son shyly hid behind her as the two adults talked. After pleasantries were exchanged, she asked her how old her son was. She said "Four, but he'll be five in June." The teacher said, "Oh, so you're going to hold him back, right?" Our friend was a bit taken aback by this. Up until this point, the mother had never considered the option of holding him out of school. The teacher continued, "I don't think your son is ready for kindergarten. Boys with summer birthdays rarely are. I think it might be smart to hold her back a year." The mother politely finessed her way out of the confrontation and went on with her business.

Still, she was upset by the exchange. She did not understand how or why this teacher made such a quick decision when just seeing her child in the hallway. She unexpectedly found herself caught in the Readiness Trap.

She went on to have discussions with other moms at her preschool and her daughter's elementary school. She also talked with the director of her son's preschool and his preschool teacher. She needed affirmation that her instinct to send him to kindergarten was in his best interest and would not be harmful to him. She was surprised by the passion that people brought to "their" side of this issue and was startled by how quickly her confidence in herself and in her son's capabilities could be rattled. Still, in the end, the director of her son's preschool and his preschool teacher reassured her that he was ready for kindergarten, and she decided to send him to kindergarten. Her son went on to have a wonderful year with his kindergarten teacher and has continued to be successful as he has progressed through elementary school.

For many of you, you have either experienced something similar to this first hand or have heard about a similar situation through a friend or family member. Either way, the idealist comments made by the kindergarten teacher in the above caused this parent to have doubts about her child's readiness as well as her skills as a mother in making the best decision for her child. This event should have never happened, but unfortunately, education reform is making the Readiness Trap wider, more severe, and easier to fall into.

School Readiness and Education Reform

Top-Down. The central issue that has driven education reform in the US since the launch of Sputnik by the Russians in 1957 is the goal of improving students' academic achievement. Which students and what types of academic achievement to be attained have continually changed since that time. Still, policymakers usually create a marker of academic achievement students are expected to attain by a specific time. This marker creates an image of accountability for government spending. Once that marker of school success is defined, a trajectory for student achievement emerges. In turn, the skills and knowledge children should possess when they enter elementary school is set. Thus, how school readiness is defined at any given time is related to policymakers' most recent public education reforms.

Bottom-Up. How school readiness is defined is not only affected by top-down policy. Preschool policy has affected this construct as well. In general, public support for funding early childhood education programs has always been contentious.[lxix] Because of this, programs such as the federal government's Head Start program have been routinely evaluated to see if they provide any lasting effect on students' academic achievement. Unfortunately, much of the intellectual gains students make from this program fade out over time,[lxx] and thus, many policymakers argue that the limited funding that does exist for public schooling should be spent on the older grades.

To counter the impact of preschool programs on young children's academic achievement, researchers in the 1980s began to look at this issue differently.[lxxi] They found that targeted preschool programs impact children's lives in significant ways beyond academic achievement (e.g., less likely to need social services, more likely to graduate high school), and these "benefits" increased exponentially by the time these children become adults. If you've heard statements such as, "Every dollar spent on preschool saves the taxpayer seven dollars," this research is where this argument emerged.

Many early education advocates, researchers, and program personnel use this "return on investment" argument to advocate for public funding of early childhood programs for children and families. For example, Nobel-laureate economist James Heckman[lxxii] has opened the Center for the Economics of Human Development at the University of Chicago. He and those with whom he works use human capital theory, a perspective dominated by the work of Adam Smith and developed by Mincer[lxxiii] and Becker,[lxxiv] to advocate for investing in early childhood programs. Such investments will save policymakers from having to make future expenditures on social (e.g., reduced rates of incarceration) and educational services (e.g., reduced participation in remedial programs). These bottom-up reforms frame school readiness as an investment in children that save taxpayers money.[lxxv]

By making the case that preschool is a good investment for taxpayer dollars, the supporters of these programs are feeding into the argument that publicly supported preschool programs have to produce children who are able to achieve academically. This in turn ties their funding to the ability of their programs to improve their students' academic achievement.[lxxvi]

It Comes Down to Academic Achievement

Both top down and bottom up early childhood/preschool reforms tend to frame the success of these programs through children who are prepared to achieve academically in school. Unfortunately, such a simple measure of success misses the complexity of the child development and learning process. It also fails to consider the impact of a range of variables on a child's preparedness for school as well as how they will develop once they enter school. Lastly, it unfortunately puts the onus for school readiness on the child—avoiding all the other variables I've highlighted up to this point (e.g., access to health care, preschool (if needed), etc.).

By putting the onus for school readiness on the individual child, many children, particularly children who are not White, middle-class, or for whom English is not their first language are deemed as being "at-risk" for school success.[lxxvii] Being labeled in such a way has been shown to deny these children the same learning experiences as their White, English-speaking and more affluent peers.[lxxviii] These learning experiences are important because they are necessary to lead children's development. Lisa Delpit,[lxxix] an education researcher, notes that there is no achievement gap when children are born. Furthermore, as Fikile Nxumalo and Jennifer Adair[lxxx] and many other educational researchers[lxxxi] have pointed out, the very idea of the achievement gap ignores the systemic sources of inequality and racism that persist throughout the US.

Placing the onus of school readiness on the child allows policymakers to ignore larger societal issues while at the same time giving them a "problem" to fix. Having problems that need to be fixed provides policymakers the opportunity to project the image that they are *DOING* something and are improving their constituents' lives. Moreover, because the focus of education reform is on addressing "particular gaps" in children's academic performance, policymakers, educational researchers, and advocates employ the idea of "fixing" particular children, families, or cultures to justify education reform or the need for specific instructional interventions in elementary schools.

So as a parent of a rising kindergartener, being aware of how the need for particular reforms in your state, district, or school are being framed or discussed in the popular media will help you see how others are thinking about your child's readiness for and success in school.

Kindergarten Entry Policies

A primary means by which policymakers influence the issue of being ready for kindergarten is the cutoff date they set for kindergarten entry. For decades, researchers in early education[lxxxii] and policymakers have been trying to figure out "when" is the optimal time for children to start school. In many states, the cutoff is September 1st, but when many of us were children, the cutoff was much later— for instance, in many states, children could enter kindergarten as long as they turned five by January 1st.[lxxxiii] This idealist understanding of school readiness, readiness being in the child, makes sense organizationally, but it is a blunt instrument for determining whether or not a child is ready for school. For example, is a child born on September 2nd quantifiably different than a child born on August 31st? Of course not, but when thinking back to the mother who thought her son had an unlucky birthday, we realize that this cutoff date carries a lot of weight in parents' minds--it might carry a lot of weight in your mind as well.

Even so, the cutoff date to enroll in kindergarten varies by state. For instance, in Texas, attending kindergarten is not compulsory but to enroll, a child must be five by September 1st of that academic year. So my middle child, whose birthday is in October, could not enroll in kindergarten until she was almost 6. In New Jersey, where two of my marvelous nieces live, the cutoff date is November 30. So if our family had lived there, my middle child could have enrolled in kindergarten.[lxxxiv]

Is Kindergarten Compulsory?

Only nineteen states plus the District of Columbia require children to attend kindergarten (AR, CT, DE, HI, LA, MD, NE, NV, NM, OH, OK, PA, RI, SC, SD, TN, VA, WV, WI); yet, almost all children in the US attend kindergarten.[lxxxv]

Once in kindergarten, the type of kindergarten program your child will attend also varies by state. Using my daughters and nieces in New Jersey as examples, kindergarten in the school district we live in Texas is a full-day program, meaning they are in school the same amount of time as a 1st grade student. For my nieces in New Jersey, they attended a ½ day kindergarten program—going to school either in the morning or the afternoon.[lxxxvi] No matter how you think about school readiness, what type of kindergarten program your child will enter will vary from state-to-state.

The Impact of Increased Student Achievement Expectations

Policymakers' reforms not only help define school readiness through how they conceptualize when children should start kindergarten and what type of program they will enter, but they also define it through what levels of academic achievement they expect children to attain at particular points in their schooling—e.g. state-based student achievement exams. This singular focus by state and national policymakers has narrowed the framing of school readiness almost exclusively to your child's ability to achieve academically. In turn, programs such as preschool or pre-kindergarten become positioned as vehicles to ready young children for school by teaching them a particular set of knowledge and skills they will need to achieve on the high-stakes exams that await them in the later grades.[lxxxvii]

I, as well as many others involved in the education of young children, worry that these reforms tend to reflect an elementary or secondary school understanding of schooling rather than an early childhood perspective.[lxxxviii] What I mean is that at the kindergarten through grade 12 (K-12) level of schooling, policymakers have implemented a series of high-stakes standards-based accountability reforms that define the success of a student through her/his ability to achieve academically on a standardized exam. In brief, these standards-based accountability reforms strive to create an aligned system of education in which all children attain a specific set of content, performance, and proficiency standards. *Content standards* list the knowledge and skills students are to learn. *Performance standards* state how students will show they have mastered the content standards, and *proficiency standards* indicate how well students must perform on the performance standards.[lxxxix] Meaning that all students within that system must demonstrate their acquisition of this prescribed set of knowledge and skills on explicit assessment measures at predetermined points in their schooling.[xc]

Additionally, every state in the US has some form of *early learning standards*[xci] in place that provide guidance for early educators in planning how they work with young children.[xcii] However, most early childhood programs, except for those receiving public funding, are not required to implement these standards.[xciii] So while early learning standards may not be a part of your child's preschool program, they do affect state and federally funded preschool programs. For instance, in Texas, state policymakers have funded a data system that can now track children's academic progress from pre-k through grade 12. This may seem to be an efficient way to measure the effectiveness of schools, but such policies raise a new set of questions and concerns about how this data might be used in relation to decisions about students, teachers, schools, and school districts.

Once children do enter elementary school, policymakers across many states have put in place a series of high-stakes reforms that tie consequences for students, their teachers, school, and/or school district to students' achievement scores on these standardized exams. The stakes are designed to motivate administrators, teachers, and students to perform better. For instance, in Texas, children's school success is defined by their literacy and mathematics achievement in grades 3 through 8. In grade 4, students also take a writing test. In grade 5, a science test, and so on. The point behind these policies in Texas and across the US (e.g., the federal government's *No Child Left Behind Act*--NCLB), is to motivate students, teachers, and/or school administrators to work harder to improve their students' academic achievement on specific standardized tests. Students' scores on the grade 5 and 8 tests in Texas determine whether they can move on (be promoted) to the next grade level. In high school in Texas, students have to pass twelve end-of-course exams across grades 9-12 to graduate and receive their diploma. What's happened in Texas has occurred all over the US. In 2010, twenty-eight states that educate 74% of the nation's students had adopted policies that require students to pass an exit exam to graduate from high school.[xciv] However, in recent years, this number has dropped to 11 states: FL, LA, MD, MA, MS, NJ, NM, NY, OH, TX, VA.[xcv]

While high-stakes assessments in the US typically do not begin until the third grade, many states as well as local school districts have responded to these reforms by putting in place a series of assessment measures across the early grades (e.g., the state-wide Phonological Awareness Literacy Screening (PALS) screening in Virginia[xcvi]). This is done to ensure children are on a trajectory for success by the time they take their state's high-stakes exams.[xcvii] For instance, 35 states and the District of Columbia implemented some type of kindergarten entry assessment. Four states had an entry exam at one point and phased it out, and nine states have never implemented such an assessment.[xcviii]

This is important because these specific points of academic achievement become the way in which many people define school readiness. These tests further define the trajectory of student achievement that children are to attain in school, and what it means to be ready for kindergarten becomes further entwined with those items found on the exams used either at kindergarten entry[xcix] or in elementary school.[c]

The Good and Bad of Testing

Still, as with any reform process, there are positive and negative outcomes that result from this shift in focus to academic achievement. The good is that there is a clearer sense of what it means for all children to be ready for school, and there is a strong willingness to ensure all children are successful in school. The bad is that this emphasis on academic achievement has redefined what it means at the policy level for a child to be ready for school.

School readiness is no longer referred to as the potential in young children. Rather, school readiness is now being defined through the ability of children to achieve academically in the here and now.[ci] This is a very different mindset when defining the ready child; it ignores the research-based understanding that children need opportunities to learn so that they can develop the skills and knowledge needed to succeed in school and in life.

How School Actors Define Readiness

Kindergarten teachers tend to frame what it means for children to be ready for school through their social and emotional skills.[cii] Parents, on the other hand, tend to focus on children's academic skills.[ciii] However, as policymakers and preschool stakeholders have sharpened their focus on academic outcomes,[civ] empirical research is beginning to document a shift in which teachers tend to prioritize children's academic skills more.[cv] Researchers, such as Wesley and Buysse, have found that this pressure by policymakers for children to achieve academically has led to school administrators and teachers "reverting to a deficit orientation in their approach to teaching in response to pressure to find what's missing and fix it fast."[cvi]

So rather than value your child for what s/he brings to the classroom, this policy environment creates a context in which school stakeholders are looking for deficiencies in your child in relation to specific academic skills in certain content areas (e.g., mathematics). Once they find these "deficiencies," they will then start working to address them almost immediately. Moreover, there is a concern among researchers that once your child has met the grade-level achievement expectations, the teacher will have to shift her/his instructional focus towards those children who have yet to meet grade level expectations.[cvii] Essentially, what these achievement expectations are doing is causing teachers to focus on their students meeting certain proficiency standards rather than the needs of their individual students. Thus, the school environment your child is entering is focused on meeting certain outcomes, and as such, the interests and desires of your child, both as a learner and as a social being, may be overlooked or not valued.

This continued escalation in academic achievement demands being placed on young children is misguided. The burden of academic success should not be placed solely on children and their families. Using Meisels' idea of the interactionist understanding of school readiness, this should be a shared responsibility in which the readiness of children is dependent on both the family and the kindergarten program they are entering.

Key Points to Remember

- Education policies for K-12 education and preschool education are focused on improving children's academic achievement.
- This top-down and bottom-up pressure puts the onus for school readiness on the child. Doing so allows policymakers to ignore larger societal problems while also providing them with a problem to fix—the gaps in children's academic performance. Such policies impact the way school readiness is framed in the context in which you live.
- Kindergarten policies (when to attend, if you have to attend, and whether kindergarten is ½ or full day) vary from state to state.
- School readiness is no longer referred to as the potential in young children. Rather, school readiness is now being defined through the ability of children to achieve academically in the here and now, which ignores the importance of giving children the opportunities to learn so that they can develop their skills and knowledge to succeed in school and life.
- Policymakers emphasis on academic achievement has led to many kindergarten teachers focusing

solely on improving your child's academic achievement in specific content areas and in regards to specific academic skills. In turn, the interests and desires of your child, both as a learner and as a social being, may be overlooked or not valued within the kindergarten classroom s/he is entering.

CHAPTER 4

What Do We Really Know about Sending Children to Kindergarten

Almost every year that I've been working in kindergarten or academia, I receive a couple of emails or phone calls from concerned family members, friends, or even people I do not know about sending their 4- or 5-year-old child to kindergarten in the fall. Below is an example of an email I received recently from a grandparent of a boy named Tommy[cviii] who was heading off to kindergarten.

> Dear Dr. Brown,
>
> I am writing because my wife and I have a 5-year old grandchild heading to kindergarten next year. For

some reason we didn't worry so much about our own kids' preparedness for kindergarten 20-25 years ago, but we are anxious about our oldest grandson's experience next year.

As a professional (lawyer), I hesitate to ask for "free" advice from another professional but figure –what the heck, worth a shot for any knowledge or guidance you may share in a minute or two –

Tommy (my grandson) seems to have a very difficult time in memorizing numbers and letters, save for a few. We and his parents have tried lots of different (fun) ways to help but still not much interest by him and what he seems to memorize today he forgets tomorrow.

He seems to be very bright, articulate, observant, and interested in lots of things otherwise, just can't learn numbers and letters! He will be an "old" 5 when he starts K, turns 6 in October.

Our daughter (Tommy's Mom) was similar and a very kinesthetic (?) learner so my wife used lots of tricks for her that seemed to work with that style. Tommy just gets frustrated regardless of the games that are tried.

So, we are concerned about what faces him in kindergarten, especially with the fairly strong changes in academic expectations that are certainly new since even our children were in kindergarten.

I am sure our concerns are no different than many (most?) parents/grandparents. And of course a google search finds lots of commentary and general advice to consider –

If you have any time at all and I understand if you hesitate to give any advice at all based on this very limited info, but I'll ask anyway:

Do you think Tommy is fairly typical for a boy and his interest will kick in? Continue to work with him as we have been? Have him 'evaluated'?

We do have a daughter of a friend who recently retired after teaching K for many years who may agree to work with him and give us an informal evaluation of how he might do in a normal K class next year –

All we are really concerned about is Tommy not getting overly frustrated with failure very early in his elementary years and the ensuing problems that may cause – want him to get a good start is all!

Anyway, thanks for listening to my concerns about our grandson! Good luck to you in your education research and teaching.

The Grandparent

Here's how I responded to Tommy's Grandfather.

Dear Tommy's Grandfather,

I understand your concerns about your grandson, but from what you've said, he sounds like a typical five-year-old to me. Since I've never met Tommy, I am very uncomfortable giving you any advice. So I think having your daughter's friend, who is a kindergarten teacher, working with him is the smartest thing to do. She'll let you know what she thinks and will probably give you advice as to how to help prepare Tommy for kindergarten.

Speaking in general terms, kids change once they get in school and interact with as well as see their peers 'doing' school. Also, I think the best thing families can do is be their child's advocate rather than worry about how they perform. Who any child is at 5 does not determine or identify who they will be in the future. Moreover, every child has strengths, and the key is to use those strengths to help him develop the areas where he needs to grow. I'll stop rambling here, but you reaching out to me tells me Tommy has a lot of people in his corner, which tells me in the long run, he'll be fine. Every child has ups and downs in school, so be careful not to let those downs define your grandchild for you.

I hope that helps.

Chris

In reading over this exchange, Tommy's grandfather wants what is best for his grandson and his daughter. Sadly, the stories he has heard, what he's seen on the internet, and the interactions he has had with his grandson have caught him the Readiness Trap. As you can tell by my response, as well as how I have approached this issue in this book, I hate that we "DO" this to parents and grandparents. As I told Tommy's grandfather, I don't want him to let others define his grandson. I also do not want others to make decisions about his grandson's education for him or Tommy's mother. Instead, I want him (and you) to be advocates for the child/ren who mean the world to you. By the end of the book, I hope you'll support not only your child but all children entering kindergarten-- that's the only way to eradicate the Readiness Trap.

By now, your confidence in deciding whether to send your child to kindergarten is growing. You have a clearer picture of what your decision entails, and it is becoming clearer to you as to what it is you want to do. So this is a good time to look at what "researchers" have found when it comes to sending children to kindergarten at particular "ages." Understanding this research will help you commit to the decision you need to make about sending your child to kindergarten. After, "we" can spend the rest of the book discussing ways you can work with your child to positively support her/his growth and development as well as prepares you for the elementary school context you are about to enter.

Understanding the Research

Overall, the research on the impact of age on children's academic, social, and sports success is mixed at best. I've heard different researchers argue that their work is definitive, but I tend to disagree with any such statement, particularly in regards to researching the impact of age on schooling. I say this because "we" are talking about your child, who is a social and cultural being entering very complex environments that vary from school to school and city to city. The schools not only act on the child, but the child also acts upon them— meaning each child's experience in the same school can be quite different.[cix]

When looking at this issue empirically, the data used and inferences made about which variables influence certain aspects of child development are very messy. For instance, to the best of my knowledge, no perfect sample of children whose parents decided to redshirt them compared to the children whose parents decided to send them to kindergarten exists. Typically, children are sorted into two groups[cx] where the achievement of a group of children born before a certain date are compared to the achievement of another group born after that date. Additionally, many of these studies are based on large data sets involving children who went to school decades ago,[cxi] which makes it difficult to understand how their experiences in schooling relates to the experiences of children in schooling today. The expectations for children in school have increased in recent years. Moreover, each data set has its limits in terms of what data is and is not there, where the study comes from (Australia, Norway, the US, Canada, Mexico, etc.), and what tools were used to measure which variable and how each variable is weighted within the statistical equation.

I am not arguing that these studies or data are worthless. Rather, you need to know that the research on when is the optimal time to send a child to kindergarten is muddy. Historically speaking, the idea of holding a child back has been seen as having a negative impact on his or her success in school.[cxii] Many of these studies focus on in-school retention such as repeating kindergarten or first grade. This research typically shows short-term gains in terms of academic achievement measures for children who repeat a grade but that repetition somehow leads to a significant increase in the likelihood that the retained children will drop out of school.[cxiii]

Moreover, a generation ago, families often saw it as a point of pride to have their child either enroll in school early (e.g., going to kindergarten at age 4) or skip a grade in school.[cxiv] In many ways, what is seen as "good parenting" has shifted and will continue to evolve with each new generation of families.

My goal in sharing this information with you is to help you be more confident in your decision. As I told Tommy's grandfather, figure out your child's strengths and growth areas, which we all have, use those strengths to help build your child's growth areas, and be a constant advocate for your child.

The research below will help you see what matters to researchers, teachers, and coaches. You can use it to support and advocate for your child—meaning, if you find out your child's kindergarten teacher is really stuck on your child being a summer birthday, shift the conversation by focusing on all the wonderful things your "young child" can do. This should help your child's teacher, who may be stuck in an idealist conception of school readiness, come to realize that s/he is failing to see your child as a "whole" person.

Moving into the Research

Preparing for the Transition to Kindergarten

An area where the research is pretty clear about how to ready children for kindergarten, no matter the child's age, is the positive impact of preparing them for the transition from home and/or preschool to kindergarten/elementary school; this preparation is done by both families and their preschool and kindergarten teachers.[cxv] For example, Schulting, Malone, and Dodge[cxvi] found using the Early Childhood Longitudinal Study, Kindergarten Cohort of 1998 data, that the number of school-based transition practices reported by kindergarten teachers (e.g., sending information home to families, teacher visits to children's homes, and parents attending a kindergarten orientation) were associated with increased academic achievement scores among children at the end of the school year. Cook and Coley[cxvii] also found that kindergarten teachers' transition practices were predictive of improving prosocial behaviors among children. Essentially, having the adults (teachers and families) supporting the children's transition into kindergarten can positively impact their academic and behavioral development.[cxviii]

Thus, it would be beneficial for you and your child to think about how you can prepare your child across her/his developmental domains for the transition into elementary school as well as how to take advantage of any opportunities your child's preschool or future kindergarten teacher may offer to help you both with this process. One way to help your child in this transition is to have your child attend some sort of preschool program for at least one year.[cxix] I am not saying that this is a necessary step for success; research has shown that over two-thirds of four year-olds have participated in some sort of preschool program (For a free chapter on what to do when your child did not go to preschool go to: https://tinyurl.com/cpb-preschool).

Additional strategies you can employ to help your child with this transition include involving her/him in some sort of peer-group activity—sports, dancing, choir, and so on. Essentially, an activity where your child is working with an adult who is not her/his parent, is not the only person working with that adult, and has to learn how to interact with peers as well as learn how to not be the center of attention.

Other transition activities you can engage in include attending an open-house for your local kindergarten program or discussing with your child what the transition into kindergarten will entail for them; this will include giving her/him a chance to ask you questions. Lastly, there are a range of books that tell stories of children[cxx] from a range of sociocultural backgrounds starting kindergarten/school;[cxxi] there is even one that talks about a teacher going to a new school.[cxxii] Such steps can make a very positive impact on your child's transition into kindergarten.

Age of Entry Research

This research examines how the relative age a child is when s/he enters kindergarten can affect a range of in and out of school variables. Before going into detail, I want to reiterate that over the past 40+ years the age of children in kindergarten has increased. One reason for this is because state policymakers have pushed the cut-off date for kindergarten entry back. For example, when I went to kindergarten, which was a long time ago, you could enroll in kindergarten as long as you turned 5 by December 31 of that year. Now, for my daughters, the cut-off date to enter kindergarten is September 1; meaning, my daughters had to be age 5 on or before

September 1. This shift in cutoff dates has been correlated with an overall increase in student performance in 4th and 8th grade, but it has shown no impact on the academic achievement of children by 12th grade.[cxxiii] Additionally, Bedard and Dhuey[cxxiv] found that an earlier state kindergarten-entry-cutoff date increases the hourly wage of males when they enter the job market, but it has no significant effect on final educational attainment. This again exemplifies how researchers are looking for statistically significant correlations in their data that you or I may have never considered when thinking about readiness for kindergarten.

The other reason the age of children at kindergarten entry has gone up is that many White, middle to upper-class families have been redshirting their children (holding them out of kindergarten for a year) for the past 30+ years. For instance, Dobkin and Ferreira[cxxv] found that in California families who enroll their children in kindergarten when they become eligible have lower income levels, lower education levels (8.9 years of schooling vs. 10.6 years) and are more likely to be African-American or Hispanic.

Many families decide to redshirt their children because they believe that if their children are older they will perform better than their younger peers in school and/or athletics as well as be better prepared for applying to college.[cxxvi] What you may not know is that while estimates of families in the United States who redshirt their children range in varied communities between 2% to 7%,[cxxvii] researchers have found that between 20%–25% of families in Australia delay kindergarten entry when children are first eligible to enroll.[cxxviii] Yet, again, researchers in Australia found that there may be a slight advantage in doing so (e.g., 1 to 2% of differences in achievement scores between younger and older children can be explained by their age in 3rd grade). However, whatever advantage there may be is gone by the time the children enter high school.[cxxix]

So Does Redshirting Your Child so S/he is Older Work?

There is research that demonstrates older children in kindergarten typically outperform their peers. However, this difference in performance, if any, levels off as children progress through school. For example, Lubotsky and Kaestner,[cxxx] who used data from the Early Childhood Longitudinal Study-Kindergarten Class of 1998–1999 and the National Longitudinal Survey of Youth-1979-Children and Young Adult Surveys that followed kindergarteners in the US, found that children who are older when they begin kindergarten score higher on tests of reading and math ability and had larger gains in reading and math test scores in kindergarten and first grade than younger entrants. These older students also appeared to score higher on various assessments of non-cognitive ability as well. However, as the sample of children in their study progressed through school,

Lubotsky and Kaestner found that after first grade, the younger entrants experienced faster growth in scores and caught up with their peers. Moreover, they found no evidence that non-cognitive skills grow faster or slower for older children. Furthermore, Black, Devereux, and Salvanes,[cxxxi] who studied Norwegian children, found that older children might have higher test scores at some points in schooling, but there are no effects on educational attainment.

Conversely, there's also research showing that being older can have a negative impact on children's school careers. Cook and Kang[cxxxii] examined student data in North Carolina and found that students who are older at kindergarten entry are more likely to drop out of school and have a higher likelihood of committing a serious adult crime by age 19. Part of this is more than likely because older kindergarteners will be 18 either in their junior or senior year of high school, and as such, they can drop out of school without parental consent. Furthermore, if they commit any crime once they turn 18, they will be tried as an adult.

I am **NOT** saying if you decide to redshirt your child that s/he will be a criminal. Rather, when looking at the research literature that has investigated this issue as a whole, what I see is a lot of researchers trying to find something *"new"* that we do not know about when it comes to age at kindergarten entry and some other measure. For example, economists Bai, Linlin, Mullally, and Solomon[cxxxiii] found that mutual fund managers who were older in kindergarten appear to outperform their relatively younger peer fund managers by about a half a percent per annum (0.48% to be exact). In other studies, there is also research that shows that older children are shown to have lower annual earnings than their peers,[cxxxiv] but the research I referred to in the above using children in Norway[cxxxv] shows that this gap appears to fade out once these individuals reach their 30s. So younger children enter the job market earlier and begin to generate an annual income more quickly, but eventually, it appears to even out.

Birth Order. Another area of investigation that researchers are beginning to pursue includes birth order. For example, Breining, Doyle, Figlio, Karbownik, and Roth[cxxxvi] found that in families with two or more children in Denmark and in Florida, the second-born boys are 20%– 40% more likely to be disciplined in school and enter the criminal justice system than are their firstborn male siblings. They think this increase in issues for the second-born is due to the role of how much time parents can spend with the first child versus the second-born child--as I tell my friends, when you have a second child, you are not adding a child, but rather, squaring a child. They also found that second-born boys tend to score lower on reading and math assessments in Denmark and on reading tests in Florida when compared to their older siblings—so maybe my own younger brother (as well as my middle child) has the right to argue our parents didn't give him enough attention.

Still, when looking at these and so many other studies not discussed,[cxxxvii] it appears that researchers are looking for issues to investigate more so than helping you decide to send your child to school.

Being Young in Kindergarten

There are some studies that have shown being younger in a kindergarten can sometimes be a disadvantage for children in relation to how their kindergarten teachers see them—I would argue it's an idealist bias. For example, in England, Norbury, Gooch, Baird, Charman, Siminoff, and Pickles[cxxxviii] found that the youngest children were rated by teachers as having more language deficits, behavior problems, and poorer academic progress at the end of the school year.

However, younger children tend to show more growth in academic skills in kindergarten and beyond. For example, Elder and Lubotsky, who studied student achievement in the US, argue that the "age-related differences in early school performance are largely driven by the accumulation of skills prior to kindergarten and tend to fade away quickly as children progress through school."[cxxxix] They contend that holding children out of kindergarten postpones learning. For instance, they argue that their "estimates clearly indicate that children's reading and math abilities increase much more quickly once they begin kindergarten than they would have increased during the same time period if they delayed kindergarten entry."[cxl] This seems to mean that being exposed to literacy and math instruction in school appears to have a stronger effect on children's skill development than holding them out for an extra year.

Furthermore, Peña's analysis of children in the state of Tlaxcala, Mexico[cxli] found that if children in school were tested at the exact same age, younger students would outperform their older classmates. However, in countries like Mexico, where all children are given their college entrance exams at the same time in school, this creates a disadvantage for younger children. In the US, taking such exams as the SAT or ACT can be mitigated by when a child takes her/his test—e.g., spring junior year versus fall senior year.

Lastly, when it comes to retaining children in kindergarten, which has been shown historically *not* to improve students' overall academic performance,[cxlii] recent research by Fruehwirth, Navarro, and Takahashi[cxliii] found retained students in kindergarten, meaning they had two years of kindergarten, learn 7% less by age 11 than they would have if they had been promoted to first grade rather than retained in kindergarten.

Yes, You Should be Confused

When stepping back and looking at this research as a whole, it is confusing and doesn't help as much as it should. To me, it shows that "we," as human beings, are resilient and our offspring can meet any challenge if we and their teachers are there to support them. If we see children as learners simply by what age they are at kindergarten entry (an idealist understanding of school readiness), "we," as parents and as teachers, are more than likely denying children the opportunity to rise to the occasion and grow and learn.

However, no matter what you decide—to send your child to kindergarten or to redshirt her/him—*make that decision based on what you know about your child and what you think will be best for her/him academically.* Moreover, make sure you have a plan to support and extend her/his learning over the next year—be it in kindergarten or a different early learning program.

I want to make one last point about this research around schooling. While it is mixed, there are nuggets that appear in this research that are of value and should get more attention that they do due to the messiness of the conversation around school readiness. For example, Dhuey, Figlio, Karbownik, and Roth[cxliv] found in their research of students in Florida's public schools that smaller classrooms in first grade appear to shrink the variance in achievement that exists between the youngest and oldest children in the classroom. These findings seem to show that if teachers are given a classroom context where they can spend more time on teaching children rather than managing them, they can help all children grow as learners. Unfortunately, when a single kindergarten teacher has to teach up to 22 five year-olds by her/himself, that teacher's focus is often on managing the class rather than having the space or time to work with children as learners.[cxlv] Thus, such research could be used by you to advocate to your local and state policymakers for smaller classroom sizes, which gets at the political side of school readiness.

Research on Children's Age and Sports

The research on being older in sports seems to be a bit clearer than the research examining age of school entry and success in school. For instance, the research with the Canadian Developmental Hockey League[cxlvi] shows a higher frequency of children whose birthday is furthest from the cut-off date not being selected for these premier teams. If your goal is to raise a star in the NHL, you might want to consider moving to Canada. Once there, you will have to come up with a plan to have a boy be born as close as possible to that cut-off date and who will love hockey as much as you. All I can say is having a family of three girls born at three different times of the year is: good luck.

The same phenomenon in regards to being older in relation to cut-off dates in particular baseball leagues (e.g., Little-League, Babe Ruth League, etc.) also correlates with an increased probability of making it into Major League Baseball.[cxlvii] Much of this has to do with the fact that coaches often mistake children's gross and fine motor development, which often appears to be greater in older children, for aptitude or talent for that sport.[cxlviii]

Since coaches gravitate towards these more developed children, this unfortunate favoritism appears to impact whether children decide to remain a part of the sport.[cxlix] For example, Furley and Memmert,[cl] who looked at male baseball and soccer coaches, found that coaches automatically associate tall players with positive performance attributes and small players with negative performance attributes. This is problematic if the goal is to identify the most gifted individuals within a certain sports population. Moreover, the son of a close friend of mine has an August birthday, and he was one of the biggest boys in his class from kindergarten through eighth grade. Yet, once in high school, most of his class not only caught up with him but passed him. The point being, the physical size of any child is a poor indicator of not only talent in sports but also for determining a child's readiness for school.

Similarly, Doyle and Bottomley[cli] and Doyle, Bottomley, and Angell[clii] found that soccer players born right after league cut-off dates are more likely to become part of an English Premier League Club because the coaches appear biased towards more mature players. However, their work also shows that these "older" players turn out to be no more talented or skillful in soccer. Thus, this poor decision-making by coaches limits the talent pool to only 43% of what might have been if all children were evaluated at the same age (meaning a lot of talented players are getting overlooked because of their age).

Still, if your decision to not enroll your child in school is based on your belief that this decision will prepare him (or her) for the major leagues, or in Texas, where the focus is still on high school football, you have to remember that even if your child makes his or her high school team, the odds of becoming a pro athlete are small. Researchers have found that boys who play baseball in their senior year of high school, have roughly 0.5% chance of being drafted and roughly a 0.015 % chance of playing in the major leagues. For football, high school seniors have roughly 0.09% chance of being drafted by an NFL team. For basketball, male high school seniors have roughly 0.03% chance of being drafted by an NBA team. For soccer, high school seniors in the US have roughly 0.08% chance of being drafted by an MLS team. For hockey, high school seniors in the US have roughly 0.4 % chance of being drafted by a NHL team. Lastly, for female high school seniors, they have roughly 0.02% chance of being drafted by a WNBA team.[cliii]

Misunderstanding the 10,000 Hour Phenomena

When looking at the research that discusses expertise, it is clear that age and when a child enters school or begins playing an instrument or sport is NOT the determining factor. Rather it's the amount of practice individuals put into that skill. For instance, the work of Howe[cliv] and others[clv] demonstrate that, "The sheer amount of training and practice a person has undertaken turns out to be the best available predictor of high levels of expertise."[clvi] This research on "work" is important because it shows that rather than believe genius, talent, or expertise is determined at birth or when your child enters kindergarten or begins playing an instrument or sport, it is something your child will develop through experience and intentional practice.

Howe, using the research of Ericsson, Krampe, and Tesch-Römer, as well as his own with Sloboda, Davidson, Howe, and Moore,[clvii] argues that it is the *sustained effort and determination* of individuals who practice at least 10,000 hours or even more depending on the skills that makes them successful. While I am not advocating that you should use this research to reign over your child's interest in any sport or skill, I do think it is significant because it highlights the importance of time and exposure to learning opportunities where, with your novice child, you are detailing and describing what is occurring. Time and exposure not only shape your child's development as a musician or athlete, but they also affect such academic skills as literacy development.

Howe's attempt to challenge how society frames what it means to be a genius is important. Howe argues that geniuses are not distinct from us, but rather, "They show us what humankind is capable of. And it is only when I acknowledge that geniuses are not totally unlike other people that our minds open up to all that I can learn from them."[clviii] What matters is providing/exposing your child with positive learning experiences that offer your child the time and space to develop her/his interests be it in academic skills, sports, an instrument, or a hobby. I am not arguing for hothousing or over exposing your child to specific activities so that they are ready for school—you'll not only burn your child out, but you might also damage your relationship with her/him.

Rather, your goal as a parent is to foster a positive approach to learning so that your child will develop an affinity for or interest in learning—Hyson[clix] calls this becoming an engaged and enthusiastic learner. Children who have a high motivation to read typically spend more time reading, which leads to them developing better comprehension skills about what they are reading, choosing more complex material to read, and feeling more successful as a reader.[clx]

None of this research can tell you whether or not your child will be successful in a particular sport, with a specific instrument, or even school. Life is too complicated to make such predictions. There will always be outliers in research where the treatment is extremely good or bad, but more importantly, there will always be participants for whom the treatment fails—be it an allergic reaction to medicine or the older child struggling to stay in school.

Moreover, there are "young" professional hockey and baseball players who do make it, which to me should be the real outliers. You also need to recognize that none of us can predict what will be the "it" job or career 20 years from now. Lastly, it's becoming more common that families have no choice in determining whether or not to hold their child out of kindergarten when s/he turns 5. School districts (e.g., Chicago Public Schools) and/or principals of schools as well as sport organizations are forcing families either to put their child in first grade if they enroll their child at age 6 or to join a specific team at a certain age.

The Impact of One's Sociocultural Background on Schooling

There is a line of qualitative research that has explored the cultural and familial practices of particular groups of children and/or child prodigies to understand what it is these individuals do to help their children succeed in school and in life. A researcher in the US that is often mentioned is Annette Lareau.[clxi] She is a sociologist who uses the work of Pierre Bourdieu to examine how one's class (economic standing) affects school as well as societal success in the US. Pierre Bourdieu, a French sociologist/theorist, documented how upper and middle class French families are able to activate, use, and transfer particular types of cultural capital to their offspring so that they will be successful in relation to institutional standards and norms. He argues cultural capital exists in three states:

> 1) Embodied[clxii]--the behavioral styles, ways of speaking, cultural preferences, and understanding of valued cultural knowledge. This capital is learned or adopted by individuals.
>
> 2) Institutionalized—the degrees, credentials, grades, and test scores that serve as social markers to indicate specific levels or types of knowledge and skills that will enable them to advance to higher levels of education and attain desirable employment and social positions.
>
> 3) Objectified--cultural goods that are owned including literature, music, art, and film as well as the sites where these are available (e.g., libraries, museums, theaters, etc.).

By being a part of a particular socioeconomic class, which I know can be a taboo word to use in the US, you are passing down to your child particular understandings of how social, institutional (including school), and cultural goods are defined, work, and can be activated. For example, you can possess objectified cultural capital by owning a painting, but you can only "consume" the painting (understand its cultural meaning) if you have the correct type of embodied cultural capital (which may or may not be transmitted during the selling of the painting). In terms of schooling, I want to be clear that Bourdieu[clxiii] did not see schools as meritocratic institutions, and as such, he argues that this false belief serves to legitimize the perpetuation of social hierarchies.

For Bourdieu, students from the middle and upper classes are more likely to succeed in school because they already possess the types of embodied cultural capital that schools value.

Annette Lareau has applied Bourdieu's insights from France to the US context. In two different studies, she[clxiv] found that middle and upper class families not only view their role in their child's education differently than lower class families, but they work to manipulate the system in their child's favor. To be clear, this is not a race issue. There were a range of "races" in both socioeconomic groups. These differences are class-based. She also compared the actions of lower and middle/upper class families outside of school. She found that middle/upper class families teach their children how to navigate successfully a range of institutional structures by preparing them for interactions with authority figures (such as doctors, teachers, or coaches) and discussing how they might address particular interactions with these adults. She termed this phenomenon as an act of "concerted cultivation" that not only teaches children "how to work the system" but also provides them with a sense of entitlement that helps them see that they have a right to "work the system" so that they can achieve their own goals and interests.

Lareau's work shows how you are preparing your child for school by teaching her/him how to operate not only within school but also larger institutional structures. So while there is a sense of confusion/messiness with the findings from the range of statistical studies that try to determine what if any choices parents can make to prepare their children for school, the work by Bourdieu, Lareau, and others show how your daily interactions with your child *do impact* the way s/he views the world as well as how s/he will respond to the challenges s/he face across her/his lifetime. Moreover, providing your child with a range of learning opportunities so that s/he can first find a personal interest and then providing them with the space to practice that skill, can provide them with the skills they need later in life.

Making Your Decision

When looking at this chapter as a whole, you can see that there's a lot here. While you are now more informed about what is and is not known about sending your child to school, the decision ultimately comes down to you and what you want for your child. Whatever you decide, you cannot regret the choice, particularly when talking with your child. I've heard numerous parents saying they wished that they had or had not held their child back. In either case, such statements do nothing but negatively impact your child.

The goal of your decision is to impact your child's school career in a positive manner, and hopefully in turn, her/his life. You need to be positive in whichever choice you make. You need to support it not only in kindergarten but for the rest of your child's life.

Remember, success in school and in life will not be determined by this one decision. For any of you who have ever watched the show *Everyone Loves Raymond*, there is an episode about redshirting (Season 4, Episode 10, "Left Back"). In it, Ray and his wife have been advised to hold back one of their twin boys by their pre-k teacher, so they decide to hold him and his twin brother back. While I don't agree with the way the teacher presented this decision to the family, I want to focus on the advice Ray receives from his father.

In the episode, Ray finds out that his mother held him back because she did not want to give up her time with him. Throughout the show, Ray is looking at this decision as if his son or he himself is "damaged" in some way, which is heartbreaking.

Towards the climax of the show where Ray is struggling both as someone who has been held back and now as a parent who needs to make a similar decision, Ray's father succinctly summarizes the messiness of this whole process. He tells Ray that he does not know whether or not they made the right decision with holding him back. He goes on to state that if they didn't hold Ray back, he might have met his wife earlier, started his career sooner, had saved more money to buy a new car faster.

The point for Ray's father (and for me in writing this book) is that no matter what you decide for your child at age 5 you will never really know whether that decision did or did not impact the trajectory of your child's life. There are too many other variables and incidents across your child's life that can positively as well as negatively affect her/his experiences in school. Whatever you decide, you need to stick to your decision and be an advocate for your child both in school and in life. Don't be wishy-washy.

Moreover, there are things you can do to prepare yourself and your child for this transition. I've written the rest of this book to help you with this task. It's time to move into helping you and your child be ready for kindergarten.

Key Points to Remember

- No matter what the "research" says, you need to be your child's advocate and use her/his strengths to help her/him succeed in school.
- The research surrounding kindergarten readiness is mixed—meaning you can find studies that support

sending children to school as well as studies that support academic redshirting/holding children out of school for a year.

- Whatever "boosts" in academic achievement appear in the early grades as the result of an "intervention," such as academic redshirting, tend to fade out over time.

- Furthermore, there are a range of studies that now measure age at kindergarten entry and how it relates to dropping out of school, high school completion, performance as a mutual fund manager and so on. The point is that researchers are looking for issues to investigate rather than helping you decide to send your child to school.

- Still, there are studies that are often not mentioned by those who advocate for redshirting children. These studies demonstrate that holding children out of kindergarten postpones their learning.

- Researchers have correlated an increased likelihood that boys born right after the cut-off dates in baseball, hockey, and soccer are more likely to be selected by a pro-sports organization.

- However, these athletes have been found to be no more talented than their younger peers. This seems to indicate that youth and high school coaches are poor decision-makers, and as such, these early decisions may limit the talent pool of the best athletes for these respective sports.

- Being a genius or expert results from experience and intentional practice.

- How you teach your child to "live" in the world, including how to make sense of school, interact with adults, and what to consume in terms of food, culture, and politics, impacts their development and success in the larger world—your daily interactions with your child and the opportunities you provide her/him with matter.

CHAPTER 5

The School Environment Your Child is Entering

One of the primary reasons you're concerned about your child's readiness for school is due to how much kindergarten specifically, and elementary school in general, have changed over the past two decades.[clxv] Kindergarten is no longer the entry point into school that teaches children how school "works," how to get along with others, and what is expected of them across the typical school day. Instead, kindergarten, as my former colleague Lisa Goldstein[clxvi] noted, is "real" school. Children come into their kindergarten classrooms and are expected to be able to demonstrate to their teachers that they can take care of themselves, interact with others, and engage in a range of learning activities. For example, kindergarteners are expected to enter their classroom on their own, put their stuff away, complete any routine tasks such as turning in their homework folder or moving a marker stating whether they brought their lunch to school or are buying lunch, and then engage in whatever type of learning experience their teacher has planned for them; this may mean doing a worksheet, reading a book, playing with puzzles, or possibly choosing one of the morning learning centers. From there, children engage in a range of learning activities with their teacher across the day, which primarily focus on teaching children specific academic skills and knowledge.

Typically, these activities are a mixture of whole group, small group, and individual activities, and most often, they are run by one teacher with anywhere from 15 to 22 students. That means your child will spend a lot of time being responsible for her/his own learning and learning routines, which includes paying attention/listening, attending to oneself and not others, following multi-step directions, being able to go to the restroom without assistance, which may or may not be in the classroom, and so on.

There are a lot of expectations by school personnel for children to be "independent," and often, that's what teachers are most concerned about the first couple of weeks of school. For example, can your child engage in the routines of the classroom on her/his own without demanding too much from the teacher or distracting her/his classmates?

An Example of Typical Day

Here is an example of what kindergarten is like based on a study I recently conducted that examined how kindergarten has changed.[clxvii] As a part of that study, I spent a semester in a kindergarten classroom, made a film about it with three different colleagues,[clxviii] and shared the film with stakeholders in Texas, West Virginia, and at the national level to see how they made sense of it. In that classroom, the children were spending a significant amount of time in whole-group, teacher-led instructional activities.[clxix] Such instructional strategies as play, center-time, and art-based activities were replaced with academic learning experiences. Below is an outline of what a typical day in the kindergarten classroom I researched looked like. The specific description of particular activities reflects what occurred in the film that was created.

A Day in Kindergarten

7:35-8:05	**Arrival, breakfast, and Pledges** (in Texas, there is also a state pledge[clxx])
8:05-8:10	**Morning meeting/Calendar**
8:10-8:30	**Phonics, sight words, and phonological awareness**
8:30-8:35	**Poetry**
8:35-8:45	**Morning Message**
8:45-9:00	**Small group word work: blue table:** Consonant-Vowel-Consonant

(CVC) bingo sheet; **red table**: Lakeshore sentence writing (noun, verb, object); **orange table:** Word Family Ladder Sheet; **green table:** Raz Kids on iPads; **Teacher's table:** CVC dice-write word.

9:00-9:45	**Shared Reading and Journal Writing at Tables**
9:30-9:50	**Read to Self and Buddy Reading**
10:00-10:15	**Snack and Bathroom Break** (tables of children are sent to a restroom down the hall from the classroom)
10:15-10:45	**Whole Group Math**: counting (days in school, backwards from 20), dot cards, number identification, number comparison, missing number, dimes
10:45-11:00	**Math Stations: blue table**: roll dice, cat in the hat counting hats activity; **red table**: Pop Addition/Subtraction game; **orange table:** Shape Pictures: sphere, cylinders, cones, and cubes; **green table**: iPads; **Teacher's table**: graph coins.
11:05-11:50	**Library**: Lesson on Plants and Seeds
11:55-12:25	**Lunch**
12:25-12:35	**Restroom Break** (whole class)
12:40-1:15	**Science Lab**: Lesson on Plants and Seeds
1:15-1:35	**Writing**: write in science Journal
1:45-2:00	**Outdoor Recess**

2:05-2:20	**Centers:** free choice, finish unfinished work with teacher
2:20 -2:35	**Review and put papers and folders in backpacks**
2:35-2:45	**Dismissal**

Take a moment to look at this schedule, it's an enormous amount of work for the kindergarten teacher and the students. Moreover, the morning is focused solely on teaching the children academic skills. It's not until the afternoon that the children have recess or center time. While not all kindergarten classrooms will have such a complex and academic schedule, many classrooms are becoming like this. As I noted before, children are racing from learning one skill to the next.[clxxi] Still, the goal of the classroom outlined in the above, and most all kindergarten classrooms, is to prepare students for what awaits them in first grade by having them develop a specific set of academic and developmental skills.

The Standardized Curriculum

Alongside these increased academic expectations for your child is the more common use of a standardized curriculum that all kindergarten teachers may use across a school, school district, or possibly, even a state.[clxxii] In many schools, districts, and even states, policymakers and school administrators are expecting every child to be taught the same academic content at a specific time in their schooling experiences. In Texas, there are schools that expect all teachers to be teaching the same content on the same day. In many instances, at the same time during the school day.

What's Wrong with This? While clearly knowing what is expected of your child in each grade level across a range of academic domains seems both informative and harmless, I have struggled with the implementation of these standards-based accountability reforms both as a teacher and as a researcher my entire career. At the most basic level, children are not widgets and standardizing them makes no sense—both developmentally and personally. This standardized system, as Julie Wilson[clxxiii] noted, operates under the "principles of control, compliance, and consumption," which means it diminishes children's confidence in themselves as learners, teaches them there is only one right answer, and frames learning as a transaction—you teach me this, I learn it and show you that I know it by taking this test.

Schools should not be Fordist-factories. They should be places that foster children's self-confidence, support and extend their curiosity, develop their creativity, encourage adaptability, teach them to be critical, and support their growth as members in a democratic learning community.

Accountability Shovedown

This push for standardization, which is also occurring in some preschool contexts,[clxxiv] is the result of what Amos Hatch termed "accountability shovedown."[clxxv] According to Hatch, content and performance expectations, as well as the didactic instructional practices of older grades, have been shoved down by administrators and others into younger-grade classrooms, including kindergarten, in an attempt to improve children's academic performance. Many have worried about the academic shovedown into the kindergarten classroom for generations.[clxxvi] However, Hatch made clear that the "current vision of shovedown" emulating from policymakers' high-stakes standards-based accountability reforms is that these policies frame learning as a lock-step process where student outcomes demonstrate the effectiveness of teachers. As a result of this, teaching practices that emphasize teaching to the whole child, which include addressing her/his cognitive, emotional, social, and physical domains through a range of instructional strategies, are being or have been eliminated from the early elementary classrooms.[clxxvii] Rather, what's happening is that kindergarten is often becoming a learning environment in which teachers must meet "prescribed curricular mandates and uniform standards."[clxxviii] These standards focus on teaching children discrete skills in literacy and mathematics that are to prepare them for achievement tests that await them in the later grades. The data from these tests are often used to measure the effectiveness of teachers and the academic capabilities of children.

The Stress of the Datafied Kindergarten

This standardization and accountability shovedown matters because what is currently occurring in many kindergartens across the United States is inappropriate. Children, families, and teachers are stressed out because everyone is focused on children meeting specific data points at certain times.[clxxix] Let me give you an example.

My amazing niece recently finished her kindergarten year in a major city on the west coast. At the end of her first quarter in school, which typically reflects one of the four nine weeks periods in a 180-day school year, my wonderful brother and his extraordinary wife had their only parent-teacher conference with my niece's kindergarten teacher. My sister-in-law and brother, like all parents, were nervous and excited. Their daughter is their only child, and this was their first parent-teacher conference in their local public school.

Just to let you know, these parent-teacher conferences typically last between 15 to 25 minutes. Their meeting lasted for 20-minutes. As you may know, as a parent, it's easy to talk about your child for much longer than that without much effort. Still, they wanted to know how their daughter was doing—was she meeting grade level expectations, was she making friends, was she happy, what's she like as a learner, etc.?

Instead, what they were confronted with was their daughter's teacher going over their kindergarten report card and their state's kindergarten readiness test, which I discussed briefly in Chapter 3. These tests are to give teachers, schools, and state policymakers a marker as to where your child "is" academically in relation to whatever skills the powers-that-be determine define the ready kindergarten. As a researcher, I don't think it is appropriate to put children in such testing situations as soon as they enter school; to be clear, a teacher does need to know where each child is at the beginning of the year, and a well-trained teacher, can do this quite easily without having to put any child in a "testing" situation. Moreover, Weisenfeld, Garver, and Hodges[clxxx] have found that these exams were originally quite comprehensive and focused on children's physical, social, language, and cognitive development as well as their approaches to learning; they now primarily focus on measuring children's literacy skills.

Still, in regards to my brother and sister-in-law, as a parent, it is nice to know where your child is performing in relation to grade level expectations. However, when looking at my niece's report card, it's data overload.

To begin, her kindergarten report card is divided into five primary categories: a) Characteristics of a Successful Learner, b) Reading, c) Writing, d) Math, and e) Other. In this large urban school district, a successful learner incorporates: Work Habits, Homework, Resourcefulness, Reflectiveness, Cooperative, and Responsible.

For the academic domains, the child is scored as: Exceeds, Meets, Close to Meeting, and Not Yet Meeting--there are no letter grades. That's a holistic score for overall academic performance.

Then, children are also scored for their overall effort in each domain as well as scored for a range of specific skills under that domain using the markers: Always Demonstrates, Often Demonstrates, Sometimes Demonstrates, and Does Not Yet Demonstrate.

For example, in Reading, my niece was given an Overall Academic Performance score of Close to Meeting. Then, for her Overall Effort in Reading, she was given a score of Often Demonstrates. From there, reading was broken into nine sets of skills, like: Separates, blends, and manipulates individual sounds in spoken words (e.g., takes apart the word cat into three sounds: c-a-t and recognizes that if the 'c' is replaced with a 'h' she would have the new word 'hat'), which she was scored as often demonstrates. Other skills included: recognizes and names all uppercase letters in random order, recognizes and names all lowercase letters in random order, produces all consonant sounds, produces all short vowel sounds, reads kindergarten text appropriately and so on.

Then, there is Writing, Mathematics, and so on, each with a range of skills children are measured in each nine weeks.

Needless to say, their first meeting with their child's teacher was overwhelming (and I am sure it was overwhelming for the teacher to collect all the data required to put together 20 or more of these report cards). My sister-in-law and brother were primarily told by my niece's teacher *what* she could not do academically. My niece's teacher told them very little about who my niece was a person or as a learner. For instance, my sister-in-law stated, "I just wish her teacher told me whether my daughter was on a trajectory for success in kindergarten, and if not, how could I support her as a learner so that she is. Her teacher really didn't seem to know my daughter as a learner and that made me very nervous." My brother also noted that he had a question about what was happening with his daughter during lunch time; he was worried because my niece seemed stressed out when he asked her about lunch time. If you're familiar with large public schools, cafeterias can be quite loud and there can be a lot of children who range in age from 5 to 13 depending on the school. Coming from a preschool environment where the 15 or so children ate together, gave thanks to the earth for their food and shared personal stories, the size and noise level of the cafeteria stressed my niece out. When my brother asked about this, the teacher did not have an answer since she did not go to lunch with the students, which is understandable since that may be the first time the entire morning the teacher has had a break. However, the teacher said she would get back to him about this and another incident but never did.

I am sharing this example not to stress you out as a parent or to make the teacher look bad. Rather, I want you to be aware of the school environment your child is about to enter. Honestly, as a teacher educator, I am concerned with how this teacher acted towards my brother and his wife; she overloaded them with data and did not appear to be aware of who my niece was as a person or what was stressful for her about school. Still, I am not surprised by her actions. The current system of public education is driven by data, and what this teacher was doing was simply mirroring what is expected of her to my brother and his wife--collecting and sharing data. Again, the point of this anecdote is not to criticize the teacher.

Instead, I want you to be prepared for the learning environment your child is entering and that means possibly being inundated with data about your child's academic achievement. However, please don't let that data overwhelm you. Instead, think about what the data does and does not capture of who your child is as a learner and be prepared to share with your child's teacher what's missing in terms of who s/he is as a learner. Remember, *learning leads to development*. I do hope my brother and sister-in-law's experiences help you think about how you might be supportive of both your child and your child's teacher too so that your child is engaged in a range of learning (rather than testing) experiences that foster her/his growth and development.

So What Makes a School Good

To me, and this is based on my experiences as a student, teacher, researcher, teacher educator, and parent, a good school is a place where the teachers are happy and the children want to go almost every day; it is a place where they feel they are learning and are seen as learners and people.

I know that's a broad answer, and from a research perspective, it's too broad. Instead, to put it in even more simple terms, what makes a good school is your child's teacher. Study after study has consistently demonstrated that the single most important factor in your child's success in school is her/his teacher.[clxxxi] The amount of time a teacher spends actually teaching your child matters[clxxxii] as well as the quality of instruction; by quality, I mean the teacher engaging in practices such as asking them questions that require them to think rather than simply parrot an answer while being engaging and empathetic to the children.[clxxxiii]

For the teacher to be able to teach in this manner, s/he must not only be a knowledgeable and competent professional, but s/he *must also be working in an environment* that is supportive and flexible. Schools that are dictatorial and directive may be able to demonstrate good test scores, but they are not good places for teachers to work or children to learn.

This ties back into my own thoughts about a good school. When you get the chance to visit your child's future school/kindergarten classroom, take a look at the people within it. Does the teacher look happy? How about the children? Alongside this, as Marilou Hyson[clxxxiv] noted, is everyone engaged in their learning environment? Are they enthusiastic about learning? Ask yourself these same questions about the larger school environment? When you walk into the school, is it a place where people seem happy and connected? Are the interactions between teachers and students positive, or is it simply a lot of direction and correction? Are children engaged in a range of learning experiences with their peers and their teachers, or are they simply sitting at desks doing worksheets? Essentially, is it a place where you would want to come back to? Or, is everyone stressed out and people seem unfriendly?

As you can tell by how I am defining a good school, I am not focused on high-standards, obedience, or control, and I am not focusing on the 3Rs (reading, 'riting, and 'rithmetic), which may be how you were educated. We need to move beyond such conceptions of schooling.

Learning is not just the basics. It is a complex personal and social process, and honestly, the so-called basics are complex; it's just that most everyone learns these things to function in society so "we" brush them aside as basic rather than seeing them for the complexity it entails to learn such skills as reading or how a base-10 mathematical system operates.

Nevertheless, we all want our children to be able to succeed in what we call "school," but we also want them to be "learners" who can tackle the unknown, problem solve, deal with discomfort in their learning/social communities, and address those "in power" when something is wrong or is not working.[clxxxv] In the next chapter, I talk about this more when addressing how to support your child in entering kindergarten and the larger public school environment.

For now, I want you to take a moment to think about where you are as a parent/caregiver.

- Are *you* ready for the unknown about your child's school generally and kindergarten specifically?
- Are *you* ready for your child to enter a place and work with a teacher that does not know your child like you do?
- Are *you* ready for your child to enter a place where s/he is going to have to be independent in ways s/he may have never been before?
- Are *you* ready for your child to enter a place where s/he is going to have to be both obedient but also be able to speak up if s/he needs help?

- Are *you* ready for your child to enter a place where s/he is not seen in the same positive/wonderful light you shine on her/him every day?

Think about your answers to those questions and where you are in relation to supporting your child through this transition into kindergarten. I am not trying to scare you here or anywhere in this chapter. Rather, knowing what kindergarten may be like will help prepare you so you can support your child as s/he grows as a learner and as a member of a learning community.

Key Points to Remember

- Kindergarten has changed since you were a child. Children are expected to come into their classrooms being able to demonstrate to their teachers that they can take care of themselves, interact with others, and engage in a range of learning activities.

- These changes are the result of accountability shovedown, which means the academic achievement expectations of the older grades have been shoved down into kindergarten.

- Be ready to be inundated with data about your child's academic achievement, but don't let it overwhelm you. Think about what it does and does not capture of who your child is as a learner and be prepared to share what's missing with your child's teacher.

- Be sure your child is entering a schooling environment where both s/he and her/his teachers are happy. If folks seemed stressed, see if there is something you can do to help them de-stress and focus on making learning a fun and exciting process.

CHAPTER 6

How Your Child Learns

When talking about how children learn or how "we" as individuals learn best, there's a myth that "we" are one type of learner: auditory, visual, kinesthetic. [clxxxvi] Scientifically speaking, that's not the case. We do have preferences for learning specific types of content in certain ways, but in reality, we learn using all of the senses we possess. Essentially, we engage our whole body in the learning process, and this is particularly true for young children.

When I say learning is a whole-body experience,[clxxxvii] remember Kagan and her colleagues' five dimensions of school readiness: a) physical well-being and development, b) social and emotional development, c) approaches to learning, d) language development, and e) cognition and general development. Their dimensions of learning provided a clearer picture as to what I mean when I say learning is a whole-body experience.

Sadly, as kindergarten has become more academic, children are offered less opportunities to engage in whole body learning experiences.[clxxxviii] This is disconcerting when thinking about the learning process for many reasons. First, because learning is a whole-body experience, children do not need to be sitting still or silent to learn.[clxxxix] Children can and do learn while moving, fidgeting, and talking with you or their siblings/friends. Secondly, there is a growing body of research that demonstrates increased physical activity in school can improve children's academic learning.[cxc] Increased physical activity has also been shown to increase executive functioning, which I discuss in more detail in just a moment;[cxci] by physical activity, I mean such activities as running, jumping, or dancing.[cxcii] Honestly, when I was a classroom teacher and knew I was going to be observed by my principal or some other school/district administrator, I would take my students out to recess beforehand so that they would be more focused during the time I was being observed—and it worked!

Think about learning as a whole body process because I don't want you to think you have to identify your child as a specific type of learner.[cxciii] Rather, I want you to spend some time thinking about what you notice about your child as s/he approaches a range of new and familiar learning and social situations that s/he typically experiences in and out of school (e.g., learning how to count as well as learning how to swim).

Here are some questions to consider:

- What sparks my child's interest?
  - Academically?
- How does my child approach a new/novel learning experience?
  - Is s/he excited, tentative, nervous, shy, etc?
- What activities engage my child's focused attention?
- How does my child react when s/he gets excited about a new or particular activity?
- How does my child react when s/he is frustrated or stuck?
- How does my child react to new social situations?
- How does my child react when an adult offers her/him help or support?
- How does my child react when s/he is corrected by an adult?

By reading over these questions, you should have a better sense of who your child is as a learner and how you might "frame" her/him as a learner when talking with others. For example, being able to verbalize to your child's kindergarten teacher that, "Jack really likes to be given the chance to try something new on his own before being given assistance. When I try to show him how to do something without giving him that opportunity, he shuts down, and it takes a few minutes for him to come back and ask to try it on his own." This is going to help the teacher think about how s/he will introduce new content to Jack as well as how to react if Jack shuts down during a learning activity. Still, I think as a parent though, it's important to understand that sometimes teachers do not have time to allow "Jack" to have a quiet moment due to the pressure they are under to try and cover as much academic content as they can in one day.

How to Think about Learning

Now that you've spent a bit of time thinking about who your child is as a learner and how s/he seems to learn best, I want to spend a moment looking at learning in a general sense. I am doing this because most of us have been "schooled" in a manner where we were told the teacher is the expert. S/he shares her knowledge with the students and that there is often one right answer that the teacher is looking for in school. Paulo Freire[cxciv] referred to this as a "banking conception" of schooling--teachers are to fill students with specific sets of knowledge and skills that they can restate/reproduce on academic achievement tests. We also believe in the myth that some children are smart and others are not. Unknowingly, we also either think this about ourselves or our children. To address these two misconceptions about the learning process,

I will first discuss how difficult learning something new really is. Then, I will talk about a better way to think about learning.

Learning is Hard

The past two decades of research have demonstrated that learning anything new is a difficult task; I am sure you already knew this, but it's important to remember, particularly when working with your child. As Daniel Willingham[cxcv] pointed out, while we, as humans, are naturally curious, we are not very good thinkers. Thinking involves using our short-term and long-term memory, specifically through our working memory, which is essentially our consciousness (what we are thinking about right now). According to Willingham, when we enter a new learning experience, we take in the information in front of us through our working memory. Then, depending on what we're asked, we pull from our long-term memory to help us make sense of the learning situation. Consider, for example, your response to being asked: what's your mother's middle name or what is the address of the home you grew up in? You would likely be able to recall the answer quite quickly but would not be thinking about that information until you were asked to retrieve it.

This process of taking in new information and making sense of it during a learning experience is a slow and difficult task that requires a lot of mental effort. Because of this, researchers have found our brains try to avoid such work.[cxcvi]

We typically try to apply what we already know to a new situation. So with your child, it is important to remember s/he has limited experiences. This means s/he also has fewer resources and memories in her/his long-term memory to apply to new situations. Therefore, s/he is going to need more support to help her/him focus, engage, and persevere as s/he works through the challenges of a new learning situation.

To help your child through this process of learning anything new, you can use strategies to support her/him including:

- Being patient.
- Recognizing the complexity in what you are asking your child to do.
- Offering your child multiple opportunities to comprehend and internalize skills and knowledge.
- Helping your child make connections with what s/he already knows.
- See if there is a pattern or schema you can provide them that will help her/him simplify the complexity of the learning activity.
- Trying to make the learning event fun and engaging, rather than a requirement, or worse, a threat.

Executive Level Functioning

When talking about how children learn, something you've probably already heard a lot about is the importance of children's "executive level functioning";[cxcvii] these functions (mental skills) form the neurological infrastructure for such non-cognitive abilities as perseverance (e.g., being able to shift and sustain one's attention), resilience, and creativity. These skills develop in our brain's prefrontal cortex, the part that controls our most complex intellectual functions, including our ability to self-regulate both emotionally and cognitively.[cxcviii] Some of these functions include maintaining information in our working memory, which allows us to keep facts in mind while working with them as well as follow multistep instructions, cognitive flexibility, such as reasoning, problem solving, and identifying/correcting errors, planning and prioritizing, and organization. Developing these skills along with the ability to self-regulate is essential for development and learning, and it takes time.[cxcix]

To be clear, you will need to do more than simply teach your child these skills or expect her/him to become intentional learners because you ask them to be; think about your own struggles when you've been put in a situation where you were "forced" to learn something new. Rather, your child's executive functions develop through having a range of consistent and supportive "learning" experiences in and outside the home. Meaning, your child will learn many of these skills from her/his interactions with and from watching you (e.g., seeing how you deal with a set-back or failure). So, having consistent and appropriate routines for your child (e.g., a bedtime routine), modeling appropriate behavior to your child (e.g., how to react when something or someone frustrates you), giving your child the chance to "redo" or correct a mistake if s/he doesn't get something right the first time (a friend of mine calls this "Giving a Redo"), and maintaining a supportive and caring relationship with her/him helps build these skills.

A Dynamic Framing of Learning

How you frame the learning process to your child matters. For me, as a teacher educator, I and many of my colleagues, try to instill in the future teachers we work with, the idea that we need to think about children and their learning through the lens of possibilities.[cc] Peter Johnston[cci] and others[ccii] calls this holding a dynamic orientation towards learning. This means children's ability to learn is not fixed; instead, they are always learning more. I believe all children will learn whatever we ask of them if given the time, opportunity, knowledge/skills, and academic and emotional support.

When we take a dynamic orientation towards learning, we are being intentional with the language we use to describe children's learning. Peter Johnston[cciii] contends that our language choices have serious consequences for our children's learning and for who they become as individuals as well as a community member. This is really important if you're trying to raise active, democratic citizens. Johnston's dynamic framing of learning hinges on the idea that we, meaning all of us, cultivate intelligence. This dynamic framing of learning contrasts with what Johnson identifies as a fixed mindset, whereby ability and achievement are seen as immutable (unchanging over time) and inherently determined regardless of instruction; simply put, who you are as a learner and your ability to learn are fixed.

Thus, by recognizing that who you are as a learner is not "fixed," but rather, dynamic, you as a parent (or as a teacher) should be aware of the words you use when talking to children about learning and who they are as learners. Your words (or the words of any adult in their lives) have the power to frame how your child sees her/himself as a learner and can influence how s/he imagines the process of learning itself.

Johnston gives the example of how one word can shape the way a child views the world or even her/himself as a learner. He notes that simply having a teacher introduce a letter-naming activity by stating, "let's see how many letters you know," versus, "let's see how many letters you know already" creates two different learning environments.[cciv] By adding the word "already," you're telling the child that "any [letter] the child knows are ahead of expectations, and, most important, that there is nothing permanent about what is known and not known."[ccv]

In brief, Johnston's work provides us with three major ideas to think about as you help your child take up a dynamic-learning framework. First, the words you use when engaging in a learning activity (or really any activity) with your child matter. For instance, how you give feedback and praise (smart vs. worked hard), or when children behave poorly or break a family rule (bad child vs. bad choice) affects how your child sees her/himself as a learner. Second, you (we all) need to think about how you frame learning. Do you think there is only one way to see the world or to learn? Do you ask your child for the "right" answer? Try getting comfortable with both different types of answers to your questions and the different ways of arriving at that answer. If your child responds to you with an answer you did not expect, ask her/him to describe her/his thinking to you and how s/he came to that answer. It not only legitimizes your child's thinking, but it also gives you insight into how your child is making sense of the world. Also, if your child makes a mistake, you need to help her see it as just that, a mistake. Mistakes can be repaired, and more importantly, they can be "learned from." Furthermore, once your child or you help your child learn from her/his mistake, it's just as important to teach your child to move on and do the next thing. As Elsa in Disney's *Frozen*[ccvi] reminds us, we need to help children learn to "let it go." Lastly, in regards to children's learning from our mistakes, and this really comes from the work of Carol Dweck who Johnston draws from in his own work, we have to recognize that children's effort in learning is not enough. We all must help children see where they make mistakes and offer specific skills instruction when appropriate so that they can move past their mistakes and become more efficient in their learning. This will help your child not only become "unstuck" but also progress toward more complicated skills and tasks.

Grit

Carol Dweck[ccvii] may be a new name for you, but she's become well known in education circles for her work on the concept of grit. Dweck defines "grit" as the ability to sustain interest (even when challenged) towards a longer term goal; some folks use the word resilience instead of grit, such as Duckworth.[ccviii] Nevertheless, Dweck points out that it is important to remember "process praise." As parents, we should praise the effort that allowed your child to complete the task or progress in her learning. We also need to teach children to question why they are failing or not making progress. Your child learning how to move forward when s/he is stuck or who to turn to for help is an important skill. Finally, Dweck makes it clear that no one has a growth mindset in everything they do all the time—this is particularly true for adults who've more than likely grown up in a fixed mindset world. This means "we" need to be aware of the triggers in our and our child's lives that can push "us" back into a fixed mindset. For example, if you've always seen yourself as performing poorly in math, being asked to complete a math task by your son (e.g., How many nickels are in $5?) can push you back into a fixed framework. Dweck contends we are all mixtures of fixed and growth mindsets, and thus, we need to help our children (and ourselves) recognize when and what led us back into a fixed mindset.

Motivation to Learn

When thinking about the learning process, recognizing the words you use play a powerful role in how you frame learning to your child as well as how your child sees her/himself as a learner. This is important because learning requires motivation (e.g., Lucille, my youngest, desperately wanted to learn how to go across on the monkey-bars on her own, just like her two bigger and stronger sisters. She did not give up for months until she could), and without it, "we" all either gave up quite easily or shut down completely. Parents can support children by thinking about learning and motivation (be it going across the monkey-bars or learning to read).

The work of two researchers, Deci and Ryan,[ccix] help make this apparent. They argue that to motivate children to learn or for children to be motivated, requires that three primary psychological needs be met. First, your child has to have a sense of autonomy, which means s/he has a sense of choice in the learning activity; another word that folks are using to define this is agency.[ccx] Secondly, your child must feel competent that s/he can complete the task at hand, which means the learning situation should be attainable but not too easy; this is a really important idea when thinking about academic learning. Finally, your child should feel a sense of relatedness to those within the learning situation, which means feeling that you, possibly her/his teacher and classmates, value and respect her/him as a learner. This highlights the significance of the social/emotional side of learning.

In their research, Deci and Ryan found that if children feel unsupported in any of these three needs, it negatively impacts their motivation and engagement with the learning experience. Thus, your goal as a parent (and the goal of your child's kindergarten teacher) should be to create an environment rooted in a dynamic orientation towards learning that offers and supports your child's autonomy, builds and supports your child's confidence, and creates a sense of relatedness. If these psychological needs are met, your child will be motivated to learn.

Learning is also a Cultural Process

While, in the US, we've often been told we live in a melting pot of cultures, research has consistently shown your culture impacts how you learn. In saying that, I am in no way saying one culture is better or learns better than another. Rather, I want you to be aware of how culture impacts the way you and your child makes sense of the world. Culture is a verb, which means that your culture (and your child's) plays an "active process" in how you make meaning of the world you live in.[ccxi] Since culture is "something to be enacted or expressed, something that is dynamic and agentic,"[ccxii] it influences how you and your child approach any learning experience--your persistence, attentiveness, and self-regulation--as well as how you approach everything you and your child do in life, including schooling and learning.[ccxiii] So just remember that child development and/or learning is not a set of skills that children acquire in lock-step order at particular times in their lives. Rather, it is a process in which children change through their "participation in the sociocultural activities of their communities."[ccxiv] Your child's development is dependent on her/his immediate experiences, which occurs within your and your child's culture.

When thinking about the school system or kindergarten classroom your child is about to enter, it's important to remember that within most institutions in the US, including schools, individualism is valued most, which might conflict with your own culture. Most of the world's cultures are more collaborative/interdependent,[ccxv] so it's no surprise that it's a big cultural shift for many students entering schools in the US for the first time.

Furthermore, research has also shown that for over 40 years[ccxvi] schools are designed for middle-class White folks. My own research around the idea of school readiness has demonstrated how kindergarten teachers often conceptualize what it means to be ready for school through a middle-class understanding of schooling. By now, this should not be surprising to you. In the article I wrote with my colleague, Yi-Chin Lan, we argued that this shift "appears to have pushed out any sort of space within the public schooling process that allows teachers to engage in instructional practices that reflect what is known about how young children develop and learn," which is disconcerting because this has led to teachers rushing "young children into academic learning. Doing so does not allow children to socially construct their own knowledge as well as limits the time for them to engage with teachers in a way that helps them come to understand what it means to be a part of a learning community."[ccxvii]

Re-centering Learning Around Your Child

Lastly, when thinking about school readiness, it's often framed from the adult perspective and how "we," as adults, try to impact each child's development--think empiricist conception of school readiness. While this is an important aspect of your child's development, the work of William Corsaro[ccxviii] reminds us that children also impact how we make sense of them and such constructs as school readiness. Corsaro, and those who take a sociological perspective towards child development, like Barabara Rogoff[ccxix] and Kundu,[ccxx] frame children as social agents within society. As such, they are constrained by existing social structures and by societal reproduction; meaning, the world in which they live impacts how they respond to it. Still, children evolve as members of their cultures by striving to interpret and to participate in them. In doing so, children create their peer worlds and cultures, and they contribute to cultural change in the larger society through their interaction with it. I point this out because I want you (and me) to remember that our interactions with children are a two-way street. Combined, our actions and the children's actions dictate their learning and development.

Again, be aware of the complexity of the kindergarten environment your child is entering, how your culture (your child's culture) affects the way you make sense of all this, and how your child might be read by her/his teacher, classmates, and other school personnel as s/he moves in and out of the school community.

Turning to Child Development and Learning

I know that since your child has been born you've been inundated with measurements, growth charts, and percentages (e.g., the height of your child in relation to typical three year-olds). When thinking about growth and development in relation to infants and toddlers, this makes sense. Your child's pediatrician is trying to identify any issues that bring to light a serious concern or possibly a developmental delay. My wife is a pediatric physical therapist, and she works with children (and their families) who face a range of developmental delays. Her goal is always to support the child now so that s/he can develop the muscle tone and coordination to move past the delay.

While there is inherent value in identifying typical trends in child development and learning, I do not want you to use this information to either revert back to a fixed framework or to assume that something is "wrong" with your child if s/he is developing differently than what is typical. Such a deficit framework can be dangerous; [ccxxi] it can negatively affect the way you see your child or, at a more global level, can be used to discriminate against whole groups of children simply because of sociocultural differences.[ccxxii]

Still, if you "feel" that something in your child's development is not progressing in the way you think it should (remember, you know your child best), do not hesitate to talk with your child's pediatrician or teacher. It is better to identify a developmental delay early on so that your child can receive the necessary therapy or services to help her/him grow beyond them.[ccxxiii] Nevertheless, remember, learning takes time. For example, as a kindergarten teacher, I saw a lot of children who were learning their letters and numbers writing them backwards (my own daughters did this too). Doing this is common as children learn this new information, and many parents would ask me about this because they were worried something was "wrong." I would tell them that it's a typical phase in their child's development, and more than likely, their child will move past it as s/he becomes more familiar with these skills. Still, "we" were both aware of this, and we worked together to make sure the issue was resolved over time.

Understanding Your Child's Development

When thinking about your child and what is often referred to as typical development and learning, which is a dynamic process, there are some things that the researchers Katz and Chard[ccxxiv] want us to keep in mind. First, there is a sequence to development. We, as humans, change over time based on our physiological development and life experiences; meaning, who the child is and how s/he experiences the world affects how s/he develops. Secondly, there is a delayed impact to development; meaning, when your (or any) child learns something new, such as how to count to ten, it may have a delayed effect on her/him that will take time to emerge. For example, as a kindergarten teacher, I never expected my students to "master" a new skill immediately. I expected them to be all over the place in terms of their ability to demonstrate what they were learning, but I also knew that they were learning, which meant I kept pushing them forward even though they might not be able to count to ten consistently.[ccxxv] Finally, there is a cumulative effect of repeated experiences on children's development, and these experiences can be positive or negative;[ccxxvi] and of course as parents, we all try to avoid negative experiences.

According to Vygotsky[ccxxvii], learning leads development.[ccxxviii] So if you have been reading to your child since s/he was born, you are not only teaching her/him the structure of language, the written word, and the process of story-telling, but you are also priming her/him to learn literacy skills such as the fluency of reading (how a story is to sound as well as the pace of reading), how the written word is read, and identifying the parts of a book (e.g., cover, title, author, illustrator, etc.).

What This All Means for Teaching Children

When transferring all these ideas into the act of teaching (learning something new is a difficult process, it takes time and support from more knowledgeable peers/adults, it must be framed through a dynamic lens, and a child's culture affects how s/he learns), it's important to remember the work of Alison Gopnik;[ccxxix] you may be familiar with her work from TV or podcasts. Through her research, she has consistently shown that children are natural born scientists.[ccxxx] Gopnik and her colleagues argue that children are consumed with the desire to experiment with and explore objects, and we, as adults, need to nurture their curiosity. For Gopnik, there are typically two ways that we talk about learning: the process of discovery and the process of mastering what we discover.

Children, as well as adults, absorb new information through guided discovery, which for Gopnik is how we increase our capacity for learning. Then through routinized learning, children perfect these procedures so that they become a part of their long-term memory, which frees their mind to make new discoveries (e.g., learning letter-sounds so that your child can focus on decoding words). Both are necessary, but unfortunately, teachers are either choosing to or are being forced to diminish the time they spend providing kindergarteners with guided discovery. Instead, they spend a lot of time on routinized learning experiences, which can either turn children off from learning or reframe learning as a process where they are told what to learn rather than see their curiosities as learning.

Furthermore, when thinking about the importance of Deci and Ryan's work on the significance of how children "feel" during the learning process, we, as adults, need to be aware of what Marilou Hyson[ccxxxi] identifies as the two socioemotional elements that shape how we/your child approached learning: our feelings (enthusiasm) and our actions (engagement). Essentially, our emotions serve as the primary motivator of our behavior, and thus, your child must be motivated by her/his emotions to engage in positive learning behaviors. Whereby, it's important to recognize that when "teaching" children anything, we need to balance our intention in our teaching between these goals of skill acquisition (e.g., learning to kick a soccer ball properly) and fostering children's dispositions towards such acquisition (e.g., seeing this process of learning to kick correctly as both beneficial and fun). If we fail to pay attention to children's feelings and emotions, we not only decrease the likelihood that children will learn the new skill (e.g., continuing to kick the ball with her/his toes), but we can also diminish their desire to learn in general (e.g., your child learning to "hate" soccer). The emotional side of learning really matters, and when thinking about all we've covered in this chapter, you now have a better sense of what I mean when I say learning is a whole-body experience—it involves your child's "mind, body, and heart."[ccxxxii]

Always talk About Your Child Through a Dynamic Framework

At this point, you may be feeling a bit overwhelmed. Having this experience is good because I want you to remember that for your child there will be several days, maybe many during the first couple of weeks of kindergarten, where s/he is going to come home mentally exhausted. Learning new information takes a lot of mental capacity and can drain anyone quite quickly. So please be sensitive to that as your child starts the new school year, and if you are feeling overwhelmed, do not hesitate to go back and read over this chapter again.

Still, this chapter has provided you with some language to talk about your child as a learner that is dynamic, positive, and rooted in a growth-mindset. More than likely, your child's future kindergarten teacher (or any elementary school teacher) is going to be overwhelmed with expectations being placed on her/him by a range of stakeholders. As such, when talking with teachers about children's learning and/or academic performance, they tend to focus on the negative or engage in a fixed language of learning. Don't be offended if this occurs but more importantly, don't fall into this trap (Oh no, another trap!).

As parents, when we do get a chance to talk about our children with their teachers, we need to remember that their teachers are good people who want to ensure that our child is successful in school. So use the knowledge you gained in this chapter about the learning process to ensure the way you talk to your child as well as to your child's teacher about learning/school is dynamic. Moreover, do not forget that learning is a whole-body experience for your child that is a slow, complex, and (can be) frustrating process.

Key Points to Remember

- Learning for children is a whole-body experience. Still, as a parent, try to pay attention to how your child attends to new learning experiences and what type of support s/he is receptive to. Sharing this type of information to your child's teachers (preschool and/or kindergarten) will be beneficial to your child.

- While your child is naturally curious about the world, s/he (like all of us) is not a good thinker. Learning is a slow process that takes time, practice, and experience. So be patient, supportive, and try to make learning fun.

- When you think about learning and development and/or your child as a learner, take on a dynamic rather than fixed framing towards learning. So think about the words you use, be comfortable with the unexpected, and help your child learn from her/his mistakes so that s/he can let them go and move forward in her/his learning.

- Also, remember that learning is not just a cognitive but also a social and emotional process. So try to create an engaging learning environment that offers and supports your child's autonomy, builds and supports your child's confidence, fosters her/his enthusiasm for learning, and creates a sense of relatedness to you and the communities in which s/he operates.

- Learning is also a cultural process and most schools frame learning from an individual rather than collectivist perspective. Depending on your cultural background and how you interact with your child, this individualistic "space" may be difficult for your child when s/he first enters it—so be sure to prepare her/him for it.

- When thinking about teaching in relation to your child's learning and development, try to foster and sustain children's curiosity by allowing them the chance to discover the world around them.

- Lastly, when helping your child master what it is s/he discovers or what you might want your child to learn in a given situation, try to do so in a way that maintains her/his enthusiasm and engagement. Once that's lost, it's time to stop and move on to something new.

CHAPTER 7

Supporting Your Child's Learning for and in Kindergarten

The expectations of what kindergarteners are to learn across the school year has changed significantly. Every state has some form of learning standards for kindergarten that define the knowledge and skills children need to learn by the end of the school year; such standards also exist for preschool too. Below, table 8.1 has links to the kindergarten standards for some states throughout the US. If your state participates in the Common Core, I would look at the California or New York documents because the standards for your state should be quite similar (41 states participate in Common Core). The other three states, Florida, Indiana, and Texas, my state, do not participate in Common Core. Nevertheless, the content and skills across all of these documents is quite similar.

Looking over these documents/content standards can be overwhelming--even for teachers. For instance, when I taught kindergarten in Virginia, I found the standards, called the Standards of Learning (SOLs), to be a list of stuff that not only did not "fit'" together, but they also did not reflect the children and families I worked with as a teacher. Still, I do want you to be aware of these standards because these documents provide you with specific insight into the academic learning that is expected to take place in kindergarten. These standards are end-of-year (often referred to as EOY) expectations; it's where your child is supposed to be at the end of kindergarten. Furthermore, in many states, the state department of education (which can be called a range of things, e.g., in Wisconsin it's called the Department of Public Instruction), often offer families and teachers numerous resources that can provide you with more insight into the standards as well as suggestions for how to support your child in attaining these EOY expectations. Also, if you want to know what your child is expected to learn in first grade and beyond, these same content standards exist for each grade level up to 8th grade. Once in high school, each state approaches content standards a little differently—some do it by grade level while others do it by content/subject area.

Table 8.1

Examples of Early Learning Standards across States

State	Content Standards
California (Common Core Standards)	https://www.cde.ca.gov/be/st/ss/[ccxxxiii]
Florida	**Language Arts:** http://www.fldoe.org/core/fileparse.php/12087/urlt/GK_LanguageArts_Florida_Standards.pdf **Mathematics:** http://www.fldoe.org/core/fileparse.php/12087/urlt/GK_Mathematics_Florida_Standards.pdf For **Science** and **Social Studies Standards,** click on the specific content area: https://www.cpalms.org/Public/ToolkitGradeLevelGroup/Toolkit?id=5
Indiana	**English/Language Arts:** https://www.doe.in.gov/sites/default/files/standards/kindergarten-ela-standards-updated-march-2020.pdf **Mathematics:** https://www.doe.in.gov/sites/default/files/standards/kindergarten-math-standards-updated-march-2020.pdf **Science:** https://www.doe.in.gov/sites/default/files/standards/kindergarten-resource-guide.pdf **Social Studies:** https://www.doe.in.gov/sites/default/files/standards/kindergarten-ss-standards-updated-march-2020.pdf
New York	http://www.p12.nysed.gov/earlylearning/documents/new-york-state-kindergarten-learning-standards.pdf

| Texas | https://tea.texas.gov/sites/default/files/Kinder_TEKS_0819.pdf |

Helping your Child Develop Her/His Academic Skills[ccxxxiv]

So now that you know more about how children learn and develop, I lay out some big ideas around the four major content areas that are typically found in elementary school: literacy, mathematics, science, and social studies. Being aware of this knowledge and skills will help you be open to learning opportunities that you can take advantage of when you are with your child (e.g., when cleaning up a room or a game, count down together from 10 and then eventually from 20 as you finish up).

By the end of this chapter, you will have a better understanding of how to help your child develop and attain these skills and knowledge in a more "holistic" or "natural" way; meaning, I am not advocating for you to use worksheets, drills, or online games to teach your child these skills. Practice is an important part of learning and using worksheets or playing online games can be a part of that process. However, what I've seen throughout my career is that teachers and some families overdo the drilling of these skills, and as such, kill their children's desire to learn new academic skills.

Literacy

For the past twenty years, I've thought about how children become literate through the work of Judith Schickedanz.[ccxxxv] For me, Schickedanz was the first to point out that English is an alphabetic orthography (a language system, both orally and in written form) where individual characters represent individual sounds/phonemes. Other languages, such as Japanese, have a syllabary orthography (a language system in which the symbols represent syllables that are blended together to make words), and Chinese is a logography (a language system where each symbol represents a word). While English is based on an alphabetic orthography, we want children to become logographic readers; they read words rather than phonemes/individual sounds; essentially, children need to learn how to break down the written word and build it back up again.

To help children achieve this goal of being logographic readers, they first need to become aware of phonemes within our language system and then build upon this awareness. So to do this, children first need to develop their phonological awareness (an awareness of units of speech such as syllables), then build phonemic awareness (manipulating individual sounds/phonemes, such as blending the c-a-t sounds to say cat), and then become phonological, and hopefully, logographic readers.

To help children become logographic readers, I draw from the work of Adams, Foorman, Lundberg, and Beeler[ccxxxvi] who have developed a useful outline of the developmental orthographic process in becoming logographic readers-- moving from simple to more complex orthographic skills.

To begin, you want to help your child first develop s/he listening skills so that s/he can make distinctions in general sounds. If your child needs assistance in developing this skill, you can help her/him by sharing interesting objects that make different noises, such as tapping on various pots or pans in your kitchen with a wood spoon, or changing the volume of your speech (speaking loud and/or soft), which helps your child become aware of the listening process.

Next, you want to develop your child's rhyming skills; this teaches her/him to distinguish between sounds that are similar and different. An easy way to do this is to share poems and sing silly songs (e.g., Raffi's *Down by the Bay*, https://youtu.be/-CSxGHve60E).

From there, you want to help your child become aware of sentences and words—remember, sentences are a set of words that express an individual thought, idea, or statement. So when you read with your child, point out words s/he is really interested in in the story. Then, show how the other words around it help make the sentences you read; this helps her/him with this process.

After your child can recognize sounds (both similar and different) and has an understanding that our language system is comprised of sentences that are made up of words, you then want her/him to become aware of syllables, which are the smaller units of speech that make up words. By playing games, such as a version of head, shoulders, knees, and toes where your child touches one body part for each syllable s/he hears, you can develop this skill.

From there, help your child become aware of beginning and ending sounds of words by doing all the above as well as using word families (e.g., -at family, which has such words as cat, bat, sat) and other word building activities that allow your child to manipulate the sounds at the beginning and end of words.

Next, work on phonemes, which refers to your child's ability to match letters to individual sound units. For example, building off of word families, ask your child what happens when you switch the 't' in tub with the 'b'—you get but, which may make your child snicker.

Once your child is comfortable with manipulating sounds and can identify phonemes, work on building back up language. This can be done through reading poems or books that are written for beginning readers. As you read with your child, you can ask her/him to help read specific sentences from the books you've read over and over again word by word. Also, writing is extremely helpful in this process. Having your child help you make a grocery list, work on writing a thank you note/email for a gift s/he may have received or letting her/him text friends and family members helps make writing purposeful and engaging for your child.

In all, there is a process to learning to read and write (and honestly, all children go through these processes differently). It is important to be aware of how the English alphabetic orthography works. If you make the process of breaking down and building up words within this system fun and engaging, you will build your child's literacy skills so that s/he can accomplish what s/he wants as a reader.

Mathematics

Whenever I talk about mathematics and children, I find people typically fall into two camps: love it or hate it. So when working with your child on mathematics, I turn to the work of Baroody and Li[ccxxxvii] who argue that the goal of mathematics instruction is to help your child develop a positive disposition toward learning and using math. This includes helping your child understand and appreciate the importance of math as well as providing her/him with experiences that engage them in the process of mathematics, such as baking cookies that use a recipe.

To assist your child in this process, make sure you're helping your child see the connection between such things as numbers and the way we use them in our everyday lives—e.g., pointing out how almost every house/apartment on your street has a number on it so "we" know who lives where. Also, when possible, help your child see how different mathematical ideas are related (e.g., the relationship between counting and addition). Lastly, Baroody and Li make the point that children require numerous learning opportunities to practice as well as explore mathematical concepts through meaningful experiences (e.g., using children's literature) and activities such as games (let's see how many steps it takes us to walk from the door to our car, and maybe the next day, try it backwards to see if it's the same or not) and/or songs (the song *5 Little Monkeys*). Furthermore, children need more knowledgeable peers and adults to be there to respond to their questions when they are confused or stuck. Honestly, math is everywhere, and we can help children recognize this as well as help them see how "good" they are at it already.

When thinking about specific mathematical skills that all children need to learn, the National Council of Teachers of Mathematics (NCTM) (http://www.nctm.org) has five strands of content that they believe children/students should learn in school to develop their mathematical skills. I touch on these briefly to help you gain a sense of what your child's mathematical learning entails.

The NCTM's first strand is number and operations, which for a kindergartener is developing an understanding of numbers and operations. This involves being able to count whole numbers, compare quantities, develop an understanding of the base-ten number system, and perform as well as explain computations in different ways. Developmentally, before your child can perform complex operations that describe change—how a quantity increases (e.g., addition) or decreases (e.g., subtraction)—s/he needs to be able to count objects meaningfully. Meaningful object counting is the effortful process that requires children to recite the counting sequence of numbers from memory (being able to count from 1 to 10) and then, being able to synchronize those words to the objects they are pointing to (counting 5 toys, which is often referred to as the skill of "one-to-one correspondence"). Finally, once your child finishes one-to-one counting, s/he must understand that the last number s/he says in the count tells how many objects there are in the set. This concept—that the last number tells how many—is known as the "cardinal principle of number," which many state standards call "cardinality" in their student outcomes. This is different from ordinal numbers, which tell you the position of something in a list--1st, 2nd, 3rd.

The NCTM's second strand is algebra. Skills that fall under this strand for young children included being able to sort, classify, and order objects by size, number, and other properties. In kindergarten, your child will learn how to recognize, describe, and extend patterns, including numeric patterns (counting by 2s--2, 4, 6, 8 …), and translate a pattern from one representation to another. Lastly, your child will learn how both repeating and growing patterns are generated.

The NCTM's third strand is geometry, which includes the ability to describe shapes and space. In kindergarten, you child will be expected to learn how to identify, name, and describe a variety of two and three-dimensional shapes presented in a variety of ways. For instance, your child will be expected to recognize a triangle is still a triangle even if the lines on one side of the triangle are longer than the lines on a different triangle. Your child will also develop and use vocabulary that locates as well as directs objects within their environment, e.g., above, below, next to, and so on. Lastly, your child will be expected to develop her/his understanding of spatial relations, which includes spatial reasoning and orientation. For instance, recognizing whether s/he can put a small square block through a round hole or putting puzzle pieces together--so working on age-appropriate puzzles is a great "math" activity that you can do together.

The NCTM's fourth strand is measurement, which includes being able to use measurable attributes, such as length, and being able to solve problems by comparing and ordering objects. Children begin to make sense of measurable attributes by first making direct comparisons between two objects to determine which is longer, shorter, taller, wider, etc. Once children see how this relationship can be applied to make indirect comparisons with other objects, they will be able to use units. In kindergarten, your child will probably first use non-standard units (e.g., cubes) and then standard units (e.g., inches) to count and assign a numerical value that tells how much of that attribute (length, height, weight, etc.) the item they are measuring has. For example, when I taught kindergarten, one homework assignment my colleagues and I gave our students was to take home a large piece of paper, draw themselves on it, and then measure themselves using one of their shoes. Then, once they brought those to school and saw how confusing it was to try to compare how tall everyone was using different shoes, we introduced using standard units of measurement with a tape measure, which made comparing heights much easier.

The final NCTM strand involves data analysis. The NCTM states that to analyze data, children must classify and organize it, represent it, and then interpret and apply the data to answer a question or solve a problem. For example, having your child sort her/his clothes by color and then saying which color of clothes s/he has the most and/or least.

None of these strands should be surprising but having a better sense of what you child will cover in mathematics across her/his kindergarten year will help you make mathematical connections to things that occur on a daily basis in your and your child's life.

Science

Let's move onto your child learning about scientific principles. Worth's (2010) argument that scientists study the world around them and beyond, and propose explanations based on evidence from their investigations—be it an experience or observation--helps define this content area in a way where "we" can see the willingness to propose, experiment, and make conclusions based on the data collected is how most children live their lives every day. Our job, as the adults in children's lives, is to tap into and foster their inquisitiveness and then connect this learning to how they are making sense of the world.

When thinking about science as a topic of study, the NRC, National Research Council[ccxxxviii] has outlined a set of key domains you should be aware of in relation to your child's learning. These domains include: science as inquiry, physical science, life sciences, earth and space sciences, science and technology, and science in personal and social perspectives, which includes discussions and activities about such things as conserving resources like water.[ccxxxix] So as a kindergartener, your child will begin to experiment with the scientific method in various ways (e.g., making predictions and then testing them out), learn such things as the different states of matter (gas, liquid, and solid), learn about how they are growing (e.g., in Virginia, we did a unit on teeth--baby and adult), and they will learn to use technology to make sense of the world as well as solve problems.

When applying these domains to instruction in kindergarten, the National Science Teachers' Association[ccxl] has identified three key principles to guide how your child should learn science. The first is that children can engage in and develop an understanding of scientific practices and principles at a conceptual level. Second, adults, including you and your child's teacher, perform an important role in helping children learn science. By providing age appropriate materials and resources as well as spurring children's investigations forward by asking "I wonder" questions, you and your child's teacher are playing an important role in children developing their scientific knowledge and skills. Lastly, just as with any type of learning experience, children need multiple and varied opportunities to participate in science activities. Doing so helps them develop science knowledge and skills through experiential learning over time in both formal and informal learning settings. Worth and Grollman (2003) note that to do this, you should provide your child with the opportunity to explore her/his world, raise questions about it, and try to answer those questions through careful observations and investigations. All of this connects to Gopnik's argument[ccxli] that children are natural born scientists, and as such, you and your child's teacher need to help her/him tap into that curiosity in a way that connects her/his curiosity with scientific concepts.

Social Studies

Honestly, for the longest time, when I heard the words social studies as an elementary school student, I never really knew what I was supposed to be learning. I didn't understand what it meant to study the "social." When I did read that the National Council for Social Studies (NCSS)[ccxlii] definition of social studies as being the promotion of civic competence among children so that they can become engaged participants in public/democratic life (NCSS, 2010), I thought, oh, so that's what I was doing all those years in school.

To help promote civic confidence among children, the NCSS has defined ten themes for organizing what they see being the key strands of social studies in schools. These strands are:

- Culture
- Time, continuity, and change
- People, places, and environments
- Individual development and identity
- Individuals, groups, and institutions
- Power, authority, and governance
- Production, distribution, and consumption
- Science, technology, and society

- Global connections
- Civic ideals and practices

These ten themes might seem a little vague, but if you look closer, these are concepts/ideas you and your child engage with on a daily basis. Think of yourself as a guide for your child as s/he comes to understand the larger social world and the history that has shaped it. To help you with this process, think about how you can make your child aware of the narratives (both historical and current) that have shaped and continue to shape your and your child's world. Also, think about what perspective has shaped that narrative (a Western, White, male perspective)? And, are there other perspectives you might bring into your child's life so that s/he is prepared to interact with others who come from different sociocultural backgrounds?

By fostering your child's civic confidence so that s/he can be an active democratic citizen, you're helping her/him be prepared to engage in and shape her/his world—for now, that's her/his immediate family and friends. Soon, it will be the kindergarten classroom, and then, the larger world. Sharing stories from yours and different cultures, visiting historical, science, and art museums, watching age-appropriate shows and movies that provide different glimpses into the world (both historical and fictional) will help your child be prepared for and thrive in the larger world.

Being/becoming an Academic Learner

The process of becoming a school learner may be easy for your child or s/he may face some struggles. The key is to be there for your child as an advocate and be supportive. As a parent, it is not always as easy as it sounds, particularly when teaching children what we, as adults, see as simple or basic skills. *Nevertheless, by being patient, using a dynamic framework, and offering a range of learning experiences to your child, you will be laying a foundation with your child that s/he will draw from and return to when s/he gets stuck in her/his learning.* Furthermore, your child will teach you more than you ever knew about who you are as a learner and how you think about learning.

Still, it's common for families to worry when their child is not learning a skill or concept they think they should know, or they worry their child will not be able to keep up with her/his classmates. I understand these worries, and if you have them, think for a minute about how much you've learned in reading this book. You now have a better sense of what to expect in terms of "what" your child will be expected to learn and how you can support such learning.

Many families look to a range of tutoring services and summer academic camps to "ready" their child for kindergarten, reading, math, and so on. I worry these tutoring services and camps are preying on your fears as a parent. They often proclaim that they can give your child a "leg-up" in school when compared to her/his future classmates. I would approach any type of "school-prep" service with caution; it is important to think about why you are attracted to such a service (pressure from a friend vs. a real concern for your child) and what you are hoping your child will gain from this experience.

Personally, I have no problem with tutoring. My wife and I have had all of our girls work with math tutors for varied periods of time when they were learning such subjects as algebra or geometry in middle school. However, we never sought out tutors for our children when they were young, particularly when it came to literacy. While learning to read young might make others think your child is "advanced," it doesn't necessarily align with what we know about how children become literate. There is a lot of research that shows the "optimal" age to learn to read is around seven, but that is often ignored in schools—mainly due to the accountability shovedown and competition I talked about in early chapters. Moreover, in many of the nations, such as Finland,[ccxliii] where children are seen as the top performers in literacy, they are often not intentionally taught to read until what we consider first grade. To be clear, you should support your child's literacy development, but please recognize literacy development (or learning in any content area) is complex and takes time. Children who want to learn to read often do quite easily. It's been my experience that for those kids who are forced to learn to read, they often resist it, which can create unbearable situations for their parents and the teacher. So, with reading or any subject area, as a parent, make learning fun and meaningful. For example, cooking is an easy way to help kids want to learn to read—e.g., reading the directions for how to cook a new recipe (particularly if it is a dessert or a treat).

Ultimately, school systems are asking a lot out of children, and in most instances, children do rise to the occasion. However, if there is a bump in the road (and as a parent of three, I know there will be), take a step back and look at the situation from a broad perspective: is it the subject, is it how your child is being taught, is your child interested in the topic/issue at hand, is what's being asked of your child reasonable for her/him, and so on. Then, if your child is in school, work with your child's teacher to develop the best plan of action forward that is attainable for you and your child.

Key Points to Remember

- Each state has a set of content standards that outlines the skills and knowledge your child is expected to learn by the end of kindergarten.
- In literacy, the focus is to help your child understand how English alphabetic orthography works. It is important to help them learn how to break down and build up the word/s.
- With mathematics, your goal should be to help your child develop a positive disposition toward learning and using math.
- In science, the goal should be to tap into your child's natural curiosity and begin to develop the skills to systematically ask questions about the world around her/him, collect data in relation to that question, and develop an explanation based on the evidence collected.
- For social studies, your goal should be to help your child gain civic competence so that s/he can become an engaged participant in our democratic society.
- Becoming/being an academic learner is an ongoing process in which your child might hit some bumps in the road as her/his learning progresses. If such bumps occur, take a holistic approach to the situation and develop an actionable and attainable plan of action for you and your child to continue to move forward in her/his learning.

CHAPTER 8

Readying Yourself for Elementary School

When sending your child off to kindergarten, there are a couple of general issues to prepare for as you embark on this new adventure with your child and the rest of your family. First, community is an important part of life, and within your community there are a range of people to talk to about any decision you make or transition you go through in your life. This includes talking with your friends, family, and neighbors about what to expect for you as your child starts kindergarten. Still, there can be certain folks who have or can make you nervous about your child's readiness for school. When interacting with those folks (think Readiness Trap here), be sure to take their advice with some caution. You are more prepared for this transition that you know, so you should be cautious with what they share with you about kindergarten. Of course, they may have valuable information that can be quite useful for you and your child but be sure not to let them try to pull you back into the Readiness Trap.

Secondly, depending on the school community you live in, you may or may not be plugged into the latest scuttle-butt about what's going on in the local elementary school. If you're planning to send your child to a parochial or private school, the community may be even larger and more difficult to manage. Nevertheless, there's often a narrative among families about what the school is like (e.g., it's great, so-so, etc.), and within that narrative, there is the conversation about which "teacher" at each grade level is the best. As a former classroom teacher and current teacher-educator and educational researcher, I can only say I would proceed with caution with these conversations.

Everyone has a different idea of what school should look like and what should happen in kindergarten. If someone tells you a certain teacher is awesome or even so-so, be sure to ask them to define what they mean. With our own children, we've heard all sorts of stories about different teachers, and while some of what we heard seemed to be true, much of it did not. The relationship you and your child have with your child's kindergarten teacher will depend on you, so keep an open-mind.

Lastly, if you find yourself involved in conversations with other parents about your child's school and/or future teacher(s), be sure *not* to have these conversations around your child/ren because they can create all sorts of emotions in your child about what her/his kindergarten year might look like. Be sure to be excited for/with your child with whomever her/his teacher ends up being. The goal is starting the kindergarten year off on the right foot and not letting others (or yourself) distract you from achieving this.

Take Advantage of the Allies in Your Child's Life

By now, your child has more than likely had a wealth of experiences with a range of adults who have seen her/him grow as a person, learner, and community member. So while this may seem like a pretty obvious recommendation, each of these adults in your child's life might possess amazing insight for not only thinking about how your child is prepared for kindergarten but also how to prepare yourself for it. If they've been in their current position/role for some time, they will have insight into what to expect from your local schools, what resources and/or folks you might look to or talk to as your child starts school. The previous families they've worked with in the past have more than likely shared with them invaluable insight into what to expect for the upcoming year. If you do have any concerns or worries about the upcoming school year, tap into the wealth of knowledge and experience these folks have about the communities you both live in.

Take Part in School-based Transition Activities

Once your child turns four, you will more than likely either start to hear of more community-based opportunities for learning about kindergarten or will be contacted by your child's future elementary school--be sure to take advantage of these opportunities. For example, within almost every school community, local elementary schools have some sort of open-house/registration activity for new kindergarteners and their families either in the spring or summer of the upcoming school year--attend these sessions. They will give you a sense of what to expect, offer you and your child the chance to visit the school together, and they will help each of you start to visualize what kindergarten is going to look like. You may or may not get the chance to see an actual classroom, and it's okay if you do not. What happens in a classroom is so dependent on the students that make up the class that even if you get the chance to visit a classroom, it's not going to tell you much about what kindergarten is actually going to be like for your own child. It just gives your child some insight into what her/his future classroom might look like.

Additionally, typically a few days before kindergarten starts, you will find out who your child's teacher is and will be invited to some sort of meet-the-teacher/open-house activity.

For instance, when I taught kindergarten, my colleagues and I would have a pot-luck dinner the Friday evening before school started in the school cafeteria to get to know families and for them to get to know us. I know that the timing of these events can be difficult to manage if you and/or your partner have to work, but if possible, I would suggest attending them. They will help you and your child feel more connected to the school and your child's teacher. Moreover, such an event can help you prepare your child for kindergarten. For example, in the classroom, you'll see where your child will put her/his coat and backpack, where her/his table/desk might be, and what materials will be available across the day. You can also spend time locating where the principal's office is, the gym, playground, etc. You can also talk with her/him about where the bathrooms are and what to expect once there (e.g., is there one in the classroom or is it down the hall?). You can also find the cafeteria and prepare them for having lunch with their classmates.

Still, if you're are unable to attend the open house/meet the teacher event, spend a little time discussing with your child what the first day might look like so that s/he is prepared for such routine tasks as asking for help, going to the bathroom, being ready for the cafeteria, how s/he will get home from school, and so on.

Some Questions to Consider as You Prepare for the Kindergarten Year

There is a lot to prepare for as your child begins kindergarten, and if this is the first time you are sending your child to kindergarten (or school of any sort), here are some questions to consider to help you and your child prepare for the kindergarten school year. (These questions are also available as a PDF at https://tinyurl.com/cpb-prepare).

- What day does kindergarten begin? (Seems obvious, but if you're planning a summer vacation, being back in town for the first day is important.)
- How long does the kindergarten day last?
- Is there a time for children to rest?
- Will there be an open house/meet the teacher event, and if so, when is it?
- What time does kindergarten start and when does it end?
- Is there a school calendar that lays out holidays, teacher work days, winter/spring break, last day of school, etc., and how do I get ahold of it?
- What will my child do on those days when there is no school?
- What is going to be "our" morning routine to get my child ready for school?

- How is my child going to get to kindergarten? Get home?
- Who are my emergency contacts if I (or my partner) am unavailable and does my child's school have this information?
- What will s/he do after school?
- What does a typical day in kindergarten look like for my child--e.g., morning, lunch, recess, end of day, etc.?
- What days are art, music, PE, library, and do I need to do anything differently on those days?
- What will my child do for lunch--will I pack something for her/him or will s/he buy food from the school?
- Is there a snack time, if so, what is my child allowed to bring?
- Where is the bathroom located and how does my child let the teacher know s/he needs to use it?
- What other adults will my child interact with across the day?

Again, some of these questions are quite obvious, but you and your child need to feel prepared. To help you answer some of these questions, you'll need to have a positive and supportive relationship with your child's teacher.

Approach Teachers as Partners

Whenever you get the chance to meet and/or talk with your child's (future) kindergarten teacher, please approach this opportunity with caution. Being a kindergarten teacher is an enormous amount of work that can often be quite stressful, so depending on when and what time of the school year these meetings occur, try to be sensitive to this. You might have a range of questions and concerns that you want to share with your child's teacher, but I would suggest holding off on those questions/concerns until you have a moment to connect on a personal level with your child's teacher. I know how stressful it is to be a parent and being overly concerned about your child is developmentally appropriate. Learn from my mistakes and try to show you not only care about your child but also their teacher as you start to build a relationship that will last an entire school year.

Also, when you do have questions for your child's teacher, be ready for her/him not to have an answer immediately available. S/he is often taking care of 20 or so children in a school with multiple classrooms and grade levels, so sometimes, the information you are looking for may not yet have been made available to her/him or s/he may not have known about whatever it is you're concerned about. If s/he is unable to answer your question, be okay with that, but do set up a time in the near future where s/he will follow-up with you via a phone call, email, or text. If s/he does not follow up, it is okay to send a kind reminder, and by then, I am sure s/he will get in touch with you.

Some Quick Tips in Talking with Teachers About Specific Incidents

Speaking of talking to your child's teacher (be it preschool or her/his future kindergarten teacher), here are a few quick tips for you if you have to talk to her/him about a specific incident involving your child or have a particular concern (e.g., Heather seems disinterested in going to school). When having to talk with your child's teacher about a specific incident or when you have a particular concern, it can be stressful, particularly if you're upset about that specific issue or incident. Nevertheless, having set out to develop a positive line of communication with your child's teacher at the beginning of the school year will make having such a conversation much easier.

Still, before you talk with your child's teacher, make sure you are in a good place for a conversation, particularly if it's an issue that makes you feel unsettled. Then, think about (and possibly write down) why you want to have this conversation and what do you hope to accomplish from this conversation with your child's teacher. Also, please remember that you may not have the entire (or even correct) "story" about the incident you want to talk to your child's teacher about; there are always *at least 2 sides to a story.* Jot down any questions you might have and be sure that what you are asking your child's teacher is reasonable--no teacher likes to get a phone call, email, text, or note from a family member saying, "We're heading out for a family vacation tomorrow, and we'll be gone for a week. If you could please send home any work you want our child to do with her/him today, that would be great."

When meeting with the teacher, please remember that being a teacher who often works alone with twenty five year-olds can be stressful. This can help you be empathetic and aware of where the teacher might be mentally. From there, share your feelings, concerns, or ideas and be sure to give the teacher time to respond to your questions. Be sure to listen and try not to interrupt, which, as a parent, was something I always struggled with because I was talking about one of the most important persons in my life, my child.

Ask follow-up questions, and then, offer to develop a plan of action with her/him. As you do that, if there needs to be some actions implemented to address your or your child's teacher's concerns, be clear about what those actions are and what "everyone" is going to do and set up a date to come back and check in with each other.

While I know this may seem like a somewhat obvious plan of action, being prepared will not only help you address any concerns/questions you might have but also ensure that you and your child's teacher are working together towards an answer or solution to your questions and concerns.

One last thing, if your first conversation with your child's teacher about a specific incident or just in general does not go well, please do not assume that your child's teacher is "bad," and more importantly, if you don't get the answers you want, please do not immediately contact the school principal. Instead, reach out to the teacher again in a few days and see if it gets better. If not, then, you might reach out to the principal for help. However, be sure to be supportive rather than critical in your conversation with the principal.

Remember, Your Child May Not be Your Child at School

Another thing to be aware of as your child enters her/his kindergarten classroom is that your child may not be the same person s/he is with you with her/his classmates or teacher(s); I think this particularly important to know if you do have to talk with your child's kindergarten teacher about a specific incident or issue. Children (and adults) act differently in different social situations, so when you do talk with your child's teacher, don't be surprised if s/he is seeing someone who is different from the child you know. I know this from experience, both as a teacher and as a parent. For example, one of my children went through a drawn-out defiance stage with my wife and me. We went to school for her first parent-teacher conference when we were in the thick-of-things, and we were expecting her behavior to be a topic of conversation in our meeting. However, the child our child's teacher described to us was a totally different person—someone who is kind, considerate, and followed directions. For us, this was a relief not only because we did not have to worry about her at school but also because it let us know that what we were experiencing was just a phase in her life.

Still, as a teacher, I've had "the other" conversation where I've told families their little angels are making some poor choices when it came to classroom behavior/interactions that did not reflect the child they knew. Luckily, we worked together to figure out what might be going on. We then developed a strategy to work together to help their child make better choices so that s/he could be successful in school.

Offer Teachers Support

Speaking both as a parent and as a former kindergarten teacher, being a supportive family to your child's kindergarten teacher will help everyone have a better year. Still, one thing that I've noticed over the past 20 years with my involvement in public schools is that "families" are not always as welcome as they once were. Some of this has to do with the increased academic demands being placed on children and their teachers, and some of it has to do with "pushy" parents who have made teachers uncomfortable.

No matter what the current landscape of parent volunteering is in your child's future school, do not be afraid to offer your support to your child's teacher. Even if the teacher seems reluctant, let her/him know *HOW* you are willing to help out (e.g., coming in, buying materials for a fun cooking activity, etc.) and that you are there to support her/him and the entire class. Please don't be a parent who is simply offering to volunteer to only work with your child or "to keep tabs" on the teacher. Such actions only create unnecessary friction among you, your child's teacher, and possibly with your child. So if you're willing, please do offer and be ready to do anything as well as be ready to do it the "way" your child's teacher asks you to do it.

If you cannot come into school as a volunteer, you should consider letting the teacher know you are willing to help do "work" for her/him at home. For example, a friend of mine helped her son's kindergarten teacher by doing such things as sorting colors of construction paper (make a red stack, blue stack, etc. out of the multi-color packs they come in) and cutting out things for bulletin boards or other projects her son's teacher was going to do with the children in class.

Key Points to Remember

- Having a plan of action for embarking on your child's first year of school will help make this transition easier for both of you.

- Maintain a positive and supportive attitude towards your child and your child's future kindergarten teacher—don't let folks distract you from this goal.

- Be sure to take advantage of the allies in your child's life to help you learn what to expect about the upcoming year.

- Also, take advantage of any school-based transition activities, like an open house or meet the teacher event.

- Be sure to approach your child's teacher as a partner who wants to work with you to ensure your child has a wonderful year in kindergarten.

- As you develop your relationship with your child's teacher, do remember that your child may not be the same person at school as s/he is at home. That's okay, and rather than dwell on it, work with your child's teacher so that s/he has a terrific school year.

- Lastly, if you're up for it, do offer to support your child's teacher in and/or out of the classroom during the school year.

CONCLUSION

Replacing Your Worry with Wisdom

Now, **YOU** can confidently answer the question: Is my child ready for kindergarten? *I cannot make this decision for you.* I do not know your child, the context and culture(s) s/he is being raised in, or the hopes and dreams you and your family have and will strive to accomplish with your child as s/he progresses through school.

You know all of these things plus what I shared with you across this book, and thus, you know whether your child is ready for kindergarten. It's now time to develop a plan of action for moving forward.

Projecting Confidence

Whatever you have decided in terms of sending your child to kindergarten, do not waiver from this decision and know that you made it with more effort and research than you had before you opened this text.

To help reinforce this decision, you need to develop what is often referred to as an elevator "speech" about your decision. Meaning, in just a few simple sentences, state your decision and why you are doing it. It can be as simple as my wife's answer to Lucy, our June 5th birthday girl, when she asked why she sent her to kindergarten: "You were ready." Or, it can be more complex, "I know my child, and he is ready for kindergarten. Moreover, there's a lot of research showing that younger children actually grow more in academic and social skills in the kindergarten year than older children. I want him to have that opportunity to grow as much as he can in school." Lastly, if you decide to hold your child out of kindergarten for an extra year, you might state, "I do not think my daughter can handle the academic pressure and social demands of a full-day of kindergarten yet, and so, I plan to enroll in her preschool next year and kindergarten the following year. I know that she may be older, which may create some unanticipated issues, but I am ready to support and advocate for her as she progresses through school." Any of these responses are appropriate and heartfelt, so take a moment and state out-loud the decision you made and why.

The Landscape of the School Environment

While hearing that kindergarten is the new first grade can be stressful, by now, you can mentally move past that narrative and think about how you and your child are prepared for what will unfold over the kindergarten year. Yes, there will be higher academic expectations than what you remember about kindergarten, probably less play and "free" time, and more demands for your child to be "independent"—both in her/his academic work and social skills. Nevertheless, you have and will continue to prepare your child for these expectations in a fun and caring way.

Being Prepared

You are prepared to send your child to kindergarten. You now have a better sense of how children learn--it's a complex and dynamic process and that learning leads your child's development in the skills and knowledge s/he will need to succeed in school and in life. Moreover, you know that when you talk about your child as a learner you (and everyone) should take on a dynamic rather than fixed framing. You also know how to locate the "standards" your child is supposed to attain in kindergarten, and you have an outline of how to support your child's growth and learning in literacy, mathematics, science, and social studies. You also know there are a range of allies within your and your child's worlds that can support as well as inform you about this transition into elementary school. Lastly, you have a list of activities and questions that can help you learn about and become a part of your child's kindergarten experience.

Still, there may be a few (if any) issues that arise during the first year of school. Maybe, at the first parent-teacher conference, you'll learn your child is not yet meeting grade level expectations. That's very typical. As with my niece, many schools are comparing where a child is at the first nine weeks in relation to where your child needs to be by the end of the year. So, once you find out where your child needs to grow, which is something we all need to do, think about how you can support her/him in a way that makes learning fun—e.g., if s/he needs growth in her/his literacy skills, sing songs, make up silly poems, play games like alphabet bingo or do short-vowel word searches, read together, and so on.

The point is not to freak out, know that your child is only five, maybe six, and learning is an uneven and difficult process that requires you to be your child's ally and biggest cheerleader. Avoid such emotions as fear, do not resort to endless worksheets or drills, avoid rewards or threats, which may provide a short term solution, but they will hinder and possibly damage the type of relationship you are trying to build with your child.

If you are really struggling, which happens to all parents at some point in the 18+ years they live with their children, take a step-back, try to think about what's really going on, what resources are available to help you understand the issue (e.g., teacher, school, friends, families, pediatrician, online, etc.) and what seems like the best plan of action for you and your child to move forward. You know yourself and child best, so don't forget that you can forge a plan to move forward.

Moving Forward

You've got this, and you and your child are going to have an amazing kindergarten year together. Having raised three daughters, I just wanted to say to please remember how special this moment in your child's life is. Over the next school year, s/he will learn so many new things and have a range of new experiences you never predicted. As with life, most will be great, but there is always a hurdle or two to overcome. Throughout this book, I've provided you with enough resources that you should be prepared for most anything.

So go forward with confidence, look for those moments that will provide you with the chance to make memories you will never forget and celebrate both the little (e.g., going out for ice cream after the first day of kindergarten) and big accomplishments (e.g., learning to tie shoes, losing the first tooth, your child reading her/his first "book").

Kindergarten is such a fun time as a parent (and as a teacher), and I wish you only the best as you get to celebrate that year of school with your child and the rest of your friends and family.

ABOUT DR. CHRISTOPHER P. BROWN

Christopher P. Brown, Ph.D. is a former preschool, kindergarten, and first grade teacher.

He is a married father of three dynamic, creative, and intelligent young women.

He is also an award-winning researcher, teacher educator, and professor of early childhood education at the University of Texas at Austin.

He has and continues to study the issue of school readiness with the goal of supporting children, their families, and teachers so that each can achieve their hopes and dreams within the schooling process.

ACKNOWLEDGMENTS

Personally, I want to thank my wife, Michele, for her belief in me and the ideas that led to this book as well as for her continued love and support over the past twenty-three years of marriage. I also want to thank our three daughters, Camille, Vivienne, and Lucille, for always reminding me what's important in life and the significance of early education in the lives of all children. I also owe a lot of thanks to all of the family members and friends in my life who have helped me get to this point in my life, including my parents, Gregory H. Brown and Margaret A. Mason.

I would also like to thank Dr. Beth Feger, Lora Templet, Jennifer Smith Enos, Dre Slaman, G. Scott Brown, and Kimberly Graben for their careful reviews and insight into earlier drafts of this book.

Professionally, I want to thank my former preschool and elementary school colleagues and the many students and their families who helped me 'live' the realities of school readiness on a daily basis as a teacher-- in particular Ruby Gordon and Susan Turner. I'd also like to thank the preservice teachers and doctoral students at the University of Texas at Austin whom I've had the opportunity to work with over the years, including Dr. Brian Mowry, Dr. Joanna Englehardt, Dr. Yi-Chin Lan, Dr. Jae Eun Lee, David Barry, Da Hei Ku, Kate Puckett, and Natalie Weber as well as many others.

I'd like to thank those who've provided with me the educational experiences that led me to think and write about school readiness and schooling in a more complex way: Dr. Peterman and Peters at Sewanee, Drs. Cahill, Theilheimer, Stiles, and Ortiz at New Mexico State, and Drs. Graue, Bloch, Price, Ladson-Billings, Apple, O'Day, Gomez, Hess, Popkewitz, Reynolds, Hassett, and many more, including fellow students and friends, at the University of Wisconsin-Madison.

Thanks to the groups of early childhood researchers and teacher educators at such organizations as the Early Education and Child Development and Critical Perspectives in Early Childhood SIGs of AERA, the National Association of Early Childhood Teacher Educators, and RECE for allowing me to share and develop my work across multiple venues and outlets. Lastly, I want to thank all of the teachers, parents, administrators, policymakers, researchers, and others who have allowed me to study what it is they do. This book and my research in general would not be possible without their generosity of time in and/or opinion about educating young children.

Finally, I'd like to thank Mike Acker for his guidance and support for this project and Dr. Kelly Henry, Emily Sander, and Dr. Colleen Murray for their continued support and encouragement in getting this book published.

QUICK REQUEST

Thanks for reading my book! I really appreciate your readership.

If you liked this book and found it helpful, could you please take a brief moment to review it on Amazon?

Simply visit http://www.amazon.com/author/profchrisbrown to select *Ready for Kindergarten?*. Then leave your honest feedback.

Reviews are extremely important to the success of a book! So, if you like what you've read (or even if you didn't), then please take two minutes to help me out with a review.

THANK YOU.

ENDNOTES

Introduction

i While I recognize the term parent can be exclusionary, that is not my intent is using this term in this book. By parent, I mean any adult who is the primary caregiver for her/his child.

ii Graue, M. E., Kroeger, J., & Brown, C. (2002). Living the 'Gift of Time'. *Contemporary Issues in Early Childhood, 3* (3) 338-353; Graue, M. E., Kroeger, J., & Brown, C. (2003). The gift of time: enactments of developmental thought in Early Childhood Practice. *Early Childhood Research and Practice, 5* (1): http://ecrp.uiuc.edu/v5n1/graue.html

iii Brown, C. P. (2010). Balancing the readiness equation in early childhood education reform. *Journal of Early Childhood Research, 8* (2), 133-160; Brown, C. P. (2013). Reforming preschool to ready children for academic achievement: A case study of the impact of pre-k reform on the issue of school readiness. *Early Education and Development, 24* (4), 554-573; Brown, C. P., & Lan, Y. C. (2018). Understanding families' conceptions of school readiness in the United States: A qualitative metasynthesis. *International Journal of Early Years Education, 26* (4), 403-421.

iv Bassok D., Latham, S., & Rorem A. (2016). Is Kindergarten the new first grade? *AERA Open, 4,* 1-31.

Chapter 1

v Brown and Lan (2018); Graue, M. E. (1993). *Ready for what?: Constructing meanings of readiness for kindergarten.* Albany: SUNY press.

vi Brown, C. P., & Lan, Y. C. (2015). A qualitative metasynthesis comparing U.S. teachers'

conceptions of school readiness prior to and after the implementation of NCLB.

Teaching and Teacher Education, 45 (1), 1-13.; Brown and Lan (2018).

vii See p. 47 of Graue, E. (2006). Teaching and learning in a post-DAP world. *Early Education and Development, 19,* 441-447.

viii Brown (2010).

ix Meisels, S.J. (1999). Assessing readiness. In R.C. Pianta and M.J. Cox (eds.), *The transition to kindergarten* (pp. 39-63). Baltimore, MD: Paul H. Brookes.

x See p. 50 of Meisels (1999).

xi See p. 52 of Meisels (1999).

xii Graue (1993).

xiii See p. 49 of Meisels (1999).

xiv I intentionally do not use the word 'weakness' in this book; I also do not use it when I teach or work with teachers or students learning to be teachers. Later in the book, I will introduce you to the work of Peter Johnston (2012) and others who advocate for a growth mindset when talking about learning and students as learners. So when using this framing towards learning, we all have strengths and growth areas (I have many, just ask my wife), and we are always working to develop those growth areas.

xv National Association for the Education of Young Children. (1995). *A position statement, revised. School readiness.* Retrieved from www.naeyc.org/about/positions/pdf/psready98.pdf

xvi Graue, E. (2011). Are we paving paradise? *Educational Leadership, 68*(7) 12-17.

xvii Strauss, V. (2016, January 19). Kindergarten the new first grade? It's actually worse than that. *The Washington Post.* Retrieved from https://www.washingtonpost.com/news/answer-sheet/wp/2016/01/19/kindergarten-the-new-first-grade-its-actually-worse-than-that/

xviii Brown, C. P. (2021). *Resisting the Kinder-race: Restoring joy to early learning.* New York: Teachers College Press.

xix Bargagliotti, A., Gottfried, M. A., & Guarino, C. M. (2017). Educating the whole child: Kindergarten mathematics instructional practices and students' academic and socioemotional development. *Teachers College Record, 119* (8), 1-41.

xx See p. 21 of Bassok D., & Rorem A. (2014). Is Kindergarten the new first grade? The changing nature of kindergarten in the age of accountability. *EdPolicyWorks Working Paper Series, No. 20.* Retrieved from: http://curry.virginia.edu/uploads/resourceLibrary/20_Bassok_Is_Kindergarten_The_New_First_Grade.pdf

xxi Bassok, D., & Reardon, S. F. (2013). "Academic redshirting" in kindergarten: Prevalence, patterns, and implications. *Educational Evaluation and Policy Analysis, 35,* 283–297. https://doi.org/10.3102/0162373713482764; Brown, C. P., & Weber, N. B. (2016a). Struggling to overcome the state's prescription for practice: A study of a sample of early educators' professional development and action-research projects in a high-stakes teaching context. *Journal of Teacher Education, 67* (3), 183-202.; Cooper, H., Allen, A. B., Patall, E. A., & Dent, A. L. (2010). Effects of full-day kindergarten on academic achievement and social development. *Review of Educational Research, 80* (1), 34-70.

xxii https://nces.ed.gov/ecls/

xxiii See p. 629 of Alford, B. L., Rollins, K. B., Padrón, Y. N., & Waxman, H. C. (2016). Using systematic

classroom observation to explore student engagement as a function of teachers' developmentally appropriate instructional practices (DAIP) in ethnically diverse pre-kindergarten through second-grade classrooms. *Early Childhood Education Journal, 44*, 623-635.

xxiv Brown, C. P., Ku, D., & Barry, D. P. (2020). "Kindergarten isn't fun anymore. Isn't that so sad?": Examining how kindergarten teachers in the US made sense of the changed kindergarten. *Teaching and Teacher Education, 90,* https://doi.org/10.1016/j.tate.2020.103029; Brown, C. P., Englehardt, J., Ku, D. & Barry, D. P. (2019). "Where's the joy in the classroom?": Families' sensemaking of the changed kindergarten. *The Elementary School Journal, 120* (2), 319-346.

xxv Dagli, U. Y., & Jones, I. (2013). The Longitudinal Effects of Kindergarten Enrollment and Relative Age on Children's Academic Achievement. *Teachers College Record, 115*(3); Duncan, G. J., Dowsett, C. J., Claessens, A., Magnuson, K., Huston, A. C., Klebanov, P., et al. (2007). School readiness and later achievement. *Developmental Psychology, 43*, 1428-1446.

xxvi Jones, D. E., Greenberg, M., & Crowley, M. (2015). Early social-emotional functioning and public health: The relationship between kindergarten social competence and future wellness. *American journal of public health, 105*(11), 2283-2290.

xxvii Claessens, A., & Dowsett, C. (2014). Growth and change in attention problems, disruptive behavior, and achievement from kindergarten to fifth grade. *Psychological Science, 25*(12), 2241-2251. ; Turney, K., & McLanahan, S. (2015). The academic consequences of early childhood problem behaviors. *Social Science Research, 54*, 131-145.

xxviii Chetty, R., Friedman, J. N., Hilger, N., Saez, E., Schanzenbach, D. W., & Yagan, D. (2011). How does your kindergarten classroom affect your earnings? Evidence from Project STAR. *The Quarterly Journal of Economics, 126* (4), 1593-1660.

xxix Duncan et al., 2007; Fryer Jr, R. G., & Levitt, S. D. (2004). Understanding the black-white test score gap in the first two years of school. *Review of Economics and Statistics, 86* (2), 447-464.

; Gutman, L. M., Sameroff, A. J., & Cole, R. (2003). Academic growth curve trajectories from 1st grade to 12th grade: effects of multiple social risk factors and preschool child factors. *Developmental Psychology, 39* (4), 777.; Halle, T. G., Hair, E. C., Wandner, L. D., & Chien, N. C. (2012). Profiles of school readiness among four-year-old Head Start children. *Early Childhood Research Quarterly, 27*(4), 613-626.; Quirk, M., Dowdy, E., Goldstein, A., & Carnazzo, K. (2017). School readiness as a longitudinal predictor of social-emotional and reading performance across the elementary grades. *Assessment for Effective Intervention, 42*(4), 248-253.

xxx Feinstein, L. (2003). Inequality in the early cognitive development of British children in the 1970 cohort. *Economica, 70* (277), 73-97.

xxxi Alexander, K. L., Entwisle, D. R., & Dauber, S. L. (1993). First-grade classroom behavior: Its short-and long-term consequences for school performance. *Child Development, 64*(3), 801-814.; Alexander, K. L., Entwisle, D. R., & Olson, L. S. (2001). Schools, achievement, and inequality: A seasonal perspective. *Educational Evaluation and Policy Analysis, 23* (2), 171-191.

xxxii Brown and Lan (2018).

xxxiii Cascio, E. U., & Schanzenbach, D. W. (2016). First in the class? Age and the education production function. *Education Finance and Policy, 11* (3), 225-250.

xxxiv Holloway J. H. (2003). When children aren't ready for kindergarten. *Educational Leadership, 60,* 1-9.; Wildenger, L. K., & McIntyre, L. L. (2011). Family concerns and involvement during kindergarten transition. *Journal of Child and Family Studies, 20*(4), 387-396.

xxxv Brown and Lan (2018).

xxxvi See p. 9 of Hatcher, B., Nuner, J., & Paulsel, J. (2012). Kindergarten readiness and preschools: Teachers' and parents' beliefs within and across programs. *Early Childhood Research & Practice, 14*(2).

xxxvii Anderson, A. T., Jackson, A., Jones, L., Kennedy, D. P., Wells, K., & Chung, P. J. (2015). Minority parents' perspectives on racial socialization and school readiness in the early childhood period. *Academic Pediatrics, 15* (4), 405-411.; McAllister, C. L., Wilson, P. C., Green, B. L., & Baldwin, J. L. (2005). "Come and take a walk": Listening to Early Head Start parents on school-readiness as a matter of child, family, and community health. *American Journal of Public Health, 95*(4), 617-625.

xxxviii Hains, A. H., Fowler, S. A., Schwartz, I. S., Kottwitz, E., & Rosenkoetter, S. (1989). A comparison of preschool and kindergarten teacher expectations for school readiness. *Early Childhood Research Quarterly, 4*, 75-88.; Lin, H. L., Lawrence, F. R., & Gorrell, J. (2003). Kindergarten teachers' views of children's readiness for school. *Early Childhood Research Quarterly, 18*(2), 225-237.

xxxix Johnson, L. J., Gallagher, R. J., Cook, M., & Wong, P. (1995). Critical skills for kindergarten: Perceptions from kindergarten teachers. *Journal of Early Intervention, 19*(4), 315-327.; Rimm-Kaufman, S. E., Pianta, R. C., & Cox, M. J. (2000). Teachers' judgments of problems in the transition to kindergarten. *Early Childhood Research Quarterly, 15*, 147–166.

xl Brown and Lan (2015).

xli Kagan, S. L., Moore, E., & Bredekamp, S. (Eds.) (1995). *Reconsidering children's early learning and development: Toward shared beliefs and vocabulary.* Washington, DC: National Education Goals Panel.

xlii Duschl, R. A., Schweingruber, H. A., & Shouse, A. W. (Eds.). (2007). *Taking science to school: Learning and teaching science in grades K-8* (Vol. 500). Washington, DC: National Academies Press.

xliii Hatch, J. A. (2005). *Teaching in the new kindergarten*, Clifton Park, NY: Delmar Learning.; Hatch, J. A. (2020). From theory to curriculum: Developmental theory and its relationship to curriculum and instruction in early childhood education. In J. J. Mueller & N. File, *Curriculum in early childhood education: Re-examined, reclaimed, renewed* (2nd ed.), (pp. 51-63). New York: Routledge.

xliv Vygotsky, L. S. (1978). Socio-cultural theory. *Mind in Society*, 52-58.

xlv Suor, J. H., Sturge-Apple, M. L., Davies, P. T., Cicchetti, D., & Manning, L. G. (2015). Tracing differential pathways of risk: Associations among family adversity, cortisol, and cognitive functioning in childhood. *Child Development, 86* (4), 1142-1158.

xlvi Bloch, M. N. (1991). Critical science and the history of child development's influence on early education research. *Early Education and Development, 2* (2), 95-108.; Burman, E. (1994). *Deconstructing developmental psychology.* London: Psychology Press.

Chapter 2

xlvii Names of people outside of my immediate family are pseudonyms.

xlviii Graue, M. E., Kroeger, J., & Brown, C. (2003). The gift of time: enactments of developmental thought in Early Childhood Practice. *Early Childhood Research and Practice, 5* (1): http://ecrp.uiuc.edu/v5n1/graue.html

xlix Rauscher, F. H., Shaw, G. L., & Ky, C. N. (1993). Music and spatial task performance. *Nature, 365*(6447), 611-611.

l Lewin, T. (2009, October 23). No Einstein in your crib. Get a refund. *The New York Times.*

li Diemer, M. A., Marchand, A. D., & Mistry, R. S. (2019). Charting how wealth shapes educational pathways from childhood to early adulthood: A developmental process model. *Journal of Youth and Adolescence,* 1-19.

lii Bedard, K., & Dhuey, E. (2006). The persistence of early childhood maturity: International evidence of long-run age effects. *The Quarterly Journal of Economics, 121*(4), 1437-1472.

liii Weil, E. (2007). When should a kid start kindergarten. *New York Times Magazine,* 46-51.

liv Gladwell, M. (2008). *Outliers: The story of success.* New York: Little, Brown.

lv Black, S. E., Devereux, P. J., & Salvanes, K. G. (2011). Too young to leave the nest? The effects of school starting age. *The Review of Economics and Statistics, 93* (2), 455-467.

lvi Morrison, F. J., Alberts, D. M., & Griffith, E. M. (1997). Nature–nurture in the classroom: Entrance age, school readiness, and learning in children. *Developmental Psychology, 33*(2), 254.

lvii Cascio, E. U., & Schanzenbach, D. W. (2016). First in the class? Age and the education production function. *Education Finance and Policy, 11*(3), 225-250.

lviii This term was coined by sociologist Robert K. Merton in 1968 (https://en.wikipedia.org/wiki/Robert_K._Merton) and takes its name from the biblical parable of talents found in the Gospel of Matthew.

lix Mac Naughton, G.. (2004). The politics of logic in early childhood research: A case of the brain, hard facts, trees, and rhizomes. *Australian Educational Researcher, 31*(3), 87-104.

lx Swadener, B. B., & Lubeck, S. (Eds.). (1995). *Children and families" at promise": Deconstructing the discourse of risk.* SUNY Press.

lxi Lin, Lawrence, and Gorrell (2003); Wildenger, L. K., & McIntyre, L. L. (2011). Family concerns and involvement during kindergarten transition. *Journal of Child and Family Studies, 20*(4), 387-396.

lxii Scott-Little, C., Kagan, S. L., & Frelow, V. S. (2006). Conceptualization of readiness and the content of early learning standards: The intersection of policy and research?. *Early Childhood Research Quarterly, 21* (2), 153-173.

lxiii Brown (2013); Brown & Lan (2015); Wesley, P. W., & Buysse, V. (2003). Making meaning of school readiness in schools and communities. *Early Childhood Research Quarterly, 18*(3), 351-375.

lxiv Claessens, A., Duncan, G., & Engel, M. (2009). Kindergarten skills and fifth-grade achievement: Evidence from the ECLS-K. *Economics of Education Review, 28*(4), 415-427.; Rouse, H. L., & Fantuzzo, J. W. (2009). Multiple risks and educational well being: A population-based investigation of threats to early school success. *Early Childhood Research Quarterly, 24*(1), 1-14.; Quirk, M., Nylund-Gibson, K., & Furlong, M. (2013). Exploring patterns of Latino/a children's school readiness at kindergarten entry and their relations with Grade 2 achievement. *Early Childhood Research Quarterly, 28*(2), 437-449.

lxv Alexander, Entwisle, and Olson (2001); Campbell, F. A., Ramey, C. T., Pungello, E., Sparling, J., & Miller-Johnson, S. (2002). Early childhood education: Young adult outcomes from the Abecedarian Project. *Applied Developmental Science, 6*(1), 42-57.; Hamre, B. K., & Pianta, R. C. (2005). Can instructional and emotional support in the first-grade classroom make a difference for children at risk of school failure?. *Child Development, 76*(5), 949-967.

lxvi Strauss (2016)

lxvii Go to: https://www.naeyc.org/our-work/families/is-school-ready-for-kindergartner

lxviii Lewis, L. L. (2019, October 8)'Redshirting' your kindergartner: Is it the right choice in the long run? *The Washington Post.*

Chapter 3

lxix Rose, E. (2010). *The promise of preschool: From Head Start to universal pre-kindergarten.* Oxford: Oxford: University Press.

lxx Westinghouse Learning Corporation (1969). *The impact of Head Start: An evaluation of the effects of Head Start on children's cognition and affective development* (ED036321). Washington, DC: Clearinghouse for Federal Scientific and Technical Information.

lxxi Schweinhart, L. J., & Weikart, D. P. (1980). Young children grow up: The effects of the Perry Preschool Program on youths through age 15. *Monographs of the High/Scope educational research foundation, 7.* Ypsilanti, MI: High Scope Education Research Foundation.

lxxii Heckman, J. J. (2000). Policies to foster human capital. *Research in Economics, 54,* 3-56.

lxxiii Mincer, J. (1958). Investment in human capital and personal income distribution. *Journal of political economy, 66*(4), 281-302.

lxxiv Becker, G. S. (1964). *Human capital: Theoretical and empirical analysis: with special reference to education.* New York: National Bureau of Economics Research.; Becker, G. S. (1975). Front matter, human capital: a theoretical and empirical analysis, with special reference to education. In *Human Capital: A Theoretical and*

Empirical Analysis, with Special Reference to Education, Second Edition (pp. 22-0). NBER.=

lxxv Reynolds, A. J., Temple, J. A., Ou, S. R., Arteaga, I. A., & White, B. A. (2011). School-based early childhood education and age-28 well-being: Effects by timing, dosage, and subgroups. *Science, 333*(6040), 360-364.

lxxvi Executive Order No. 13, 563, 76 F.R. 3821 (2011) Available at: http://federalregister.gov/a/2011-1385 (accessed 12 January 2012).

lxxvii Nxumalo, F., & Brown, C. P. (Eds.). (2019). *Disrupting and countering deficits in early childhood education.* New York: Routledge.

lxxviii Adair, J. K., Colgrove, K. S. S., & McManus, M. E. (2018). Troubling messages: Agency and learning in the early schooling experiences of children of Latinx immigrants. *Teachers College Record, 120,* 1-40.; Souto-Manning, M. (2018). Disrupting Eurocentric epistemologies: Re-mediating transitions to centre intersectionally-minoritised immigrant children, families and communities. *European Journal of Education, 53,* 456-468.

lxxix Delpit, L. D. (2012). *"Multiplication is for white people": Raising expectations for other people's children.* New York: The New Press.

lxxx Nxumalo, F., & Adair, J. K. (2019). Social justice and equity in early childhood education. In C. P.. Brown, M. B. McMullen, & N. File (Eds.), *The Wiley handbook of early childhood care and education* (pp. 661-682). Somerset, NJ: Wiley Blackwell.

lxxxi Valencia, R. R. (1997). *The evolution of deficit thinking: Educational thought and practices.* New York: Routledge.

lxxxii Shepard, L. A., & Smith, M. L. (1986). School readiness and kindergarten retention: A policy analysis. *Educational Leadership, 44*(3), 78-86.

lxxxiii Elder, T. E., & Lubotsky, D. H. (2009). Kindergarten entrance age and children's achievement impacts of state policies, family background, and peers. *Journal of Human Resources, 44* (3), 641-683.

lxxxiv Go to the Education Commission of the States web page on Access to Kindergarten to see a complete list of the age cutoff as well as the age at which school becomes compulsory for young children (http://mb2.ecs.org/reports/Report.aspx?id=32)

lxxxv Kelley, B., Weyer, M., McCann, M., Brown, S., & Keily, T. (2020). *50 state comparison: State K-3 policies.* Washington, DC: Education Commission of the States. Retrieved from: http://www.ecs.org/kindergarten-policies/

lxxxvi Seventeen states (AR, CT, DE, HI, LA, MD, NV, NM, OH, OK, RI, SC, SD, TN, VA, WV, WI), plus the District of Columbia, require school districts to offer full day kindergarten.

lxxxvii Brown, C. P. (2009b). Being accountable for one's own governing: A case study of early

educators responding to standards-based early childhood education reform. *Contemporary Issues in Early Childhood, 10* (1), 3-23.

lxxxviii Ryan, S. (2008). Action or reaction! Reflecting on Sally Lubeck's wisdom to reinvent the field of early education. *Journal of Early Childhood Research,* 6(1), 69-74.; Scott-Little, Kagan, and Frelow (2006).

lxxxix O'Day, J. A. (2002). Complexity, accountability, and school improvement. *Harvard Educational Review, 72,* 293-329.; Resnick, L., & Zurawsky, C. (2005). Getting back on course. *American Educator, 29*(1), 8-46.

xc Elmore, 2003; Linn, 2000 Elmore, R. F. (2003). The challenges of accountability. *Educational Leadership, 61*(3), 6-10.; Linn, R. L. (2000). Assessments and accountability. *Educational researcher, 29*(2), 4-16.

xci See https://childcareta.acf.hhs.gov/resource/state-early-learning-standards-and-guidelines

xcii Daily, S., Burkhauser, M., & Halle, T. (2010). A Review of School Readiness Practices in the States: Early Learning Guidelines and Assessments. Early Childhood Highlights. Volume 1, Issue 3. *Child Trends.*

xciii Scott-Little, C., Kagan, S. L., Frelow, V. S., & Reid, J. (2008). Inside the content of infant-toddler early learning guidelines: Results from analyses, issues to consider, and recommendations. *Greensboro, NC: University of North Carolina at Greensboro.*

xciv Dietz , S. (2010). *State high school tests: Exit exams and other assessments* . Washington , DC : Center on Education Policy .

xcv Go to http://www.fairtest.org/graduation-test-update-states-recently-eliminated#:~:text=States%20that%20have%20graduation%20tests,Virginia%2C%20a%20total%20of%2011

xcvi Go to http://pals.virginia.edu/ to learn more about the PALS

xcvii Booher-Jennings, J. (2005). Below the bubble: "Educational triage" and the Texas accountability system. *American Educational Research Journal, 42*(2), 231-268.

xcviii Weisenfeld, G. G., Garver, K., & Hodges, K. (2020): Federal and state efforts in the implementation of kindergarten entry assessments (2011-2018). *Early Education and Development, 31*(5), 632-652.

xcix Weisenfeld et al. (2020)

c Hatch, J. A. and Grieshaber, S. (2002). Child observation and accountability in early childhood education: Perspectives from Australia and the United States. *Early Childhood Education Journal,* 29(4): 227–231.

ci Brown, C. P. (2015). Conforming to reform: Teaching pre-kindergarten in a neoliberal early education system. *Journal of Early Childhood Research, 13,* 236-251.

cii Hains et al. (1989); Lin et al. (2003)

ciii Diamond, K. E., Reagan, A. J., & Bandyk, J. E. (2000). Parents' conceptions of kindergarten readiness: Relationships with race, ethnicity, and development. *The Journal of Educational Research, 94*(2), 93-100.

civ Brown, C. P. (2007). Unpacking standards in early childhood education. *Teachers College Record, 109* (3), 635-668.

cv Adcock, S. G., & Patton, M. M. (2001). Views of effective early childhood educators regarding systemic constraints that affect their teaching. *Journal of Research in Childhood Education, 15*(2), 194-208.; Brown and Lan (2015; 2018).

cvi See p. 369 of Wesley and Buysse (2003).

cvii Booher-Jennings (2006); Gillborn, D., & Youdell, D. (2000). *Rationing education.* Buckingham: Open University Press.

Chapter 4

cviii All names are pseudonyms

cix Bronfenbrenner, U. (1979). *The ecology of human development.* Cambridge: Harvard University Press.

cx DeCicca, P., & Smith, J. (2013). The long-run impacts of early childhood education: Evidence from a failed policy experiment. *Economics of Education Review, 36,* 41-59.

cxi Babcock, P., & Bedard, K. (2011). The wages of failure: New evidence on school retention and long-run outcomes. *Education Finance and Policy, 6* (3), 293-322.

cxii Graue, E., & DiPerna, J. (2000). Redshirting and early retention: Who gets the "gift of time" and what are its outcomes? American Educational Research Journal, 37, 509–534.; Holmes, C. T. (1989). Grade level retention effects: A meta-analysis of research studies. *Flunking grades: Research and Policies on Retention, 16,* 33.

cxiii Alexander et al. (2000); Rumberger, R. W. (1995). Dropping out of middle school: A multilevel analysis of students and schools. *American Educational Research Journal, 32*(3), 583-625.

cxiv Flanagan, L. (2017, January 23). Are kids missing out by not skipping a grade? KQED. Retrieved from: https://www.kqed.org/mindshift/47119/are-kids-missing-out-by-not-skipping-a-grade

cxv Ferretti, L. K., & Bub, K. L. (2017). Family routines and school readiness during the transition to kindergarten. *Early Education and Development, 28*(1), 59-77.

cxvi Schulting, A. B., Malone, P. S., & Dodge, K. A. (2005). The effect of school-based kindergarten transition policies and practices on child academic outcomes. *Developmental Psychology, 41,* 860-871.

cxvii Cook, K. D., & Coley, R. L. (2017). School transition practices and children's social and academic adjustment in kindergarten. *Journal of Educational Psychology, 109*(2), 166-177.

cxviii Pianta, R. C., & Kraft-Sayre, M. (2003). Successful kindergarten transition: Your guide to connecting children, families, and schools. Baltimore, MD: Brookes.; Rimm-Kaufman, S. E., Pianta, R. C., & Cox, M. J. (2000). Teachers' judgments of problems in the transition to kindergarten. *Early Childhood Research Quarterly, 15*, 147–166.; Winsler, A., Tran, H., Hartman, S. C., Madigan, A. L., Manfra, L., & Bleiker, C. (2008). School readiness gains made by ethnically diverse children in poverty attending center-based childcare and public school pre-kindergarten programs. *Early Childhood Research Quarterly, 23*(3), 314-329.

cxix Cornelissen, T., & Dustmann, C. (2019). Early school exposure, test scores, and noncognitive outcomes. *American Economic Journal: Economic Policy, 11*(2), 35-63.

cxx Steinberg, D. J., & Chambers, M. (2012). *Kindergarten, here I come!* New York: Grosset & Dunlap.

cxxi Derby, S. & Song, M. (2017). *A new school year: Stories in 6 voices.* Watertown, MA: Charlesbridge.; Woodson, J. & López, R. (2018). *The day you begin.* New York: Penguin Random House.

cxxii Danneberg, J. (2000). *First day jitters.* Watertown, MA: Charlesbridge.

cxxiii Fletcher, J., & Kim, T. (2016). The effects of changes in kindergarten entry age policies on educational achievement. *Economics of Education Review, 50*, 45-62.

cxxiv Bedard, K., & Dhuey, E. (2012). School-entry policies and skill accumulation across directly and indirectly affected individuals. *Journal of Human Resources, 47* (3), 643-683.

cxxv Dobkin, C., & Ferreira, F. (2010). Do school entry laws affect educational attainment and labor market outcomes?. *Economics of Education Review, 29*(1), 40-54.

cxxvi Weil (2007).

cxxvii Bassok and Reardon (2013); Fortner, C. K., & Jenkins, J. M. (2017). Kindergarten redshirting: Motivations and spillovers using census-level data. *Early Childhood Research Quarterly, 38*, 44-56.; Graue and DiPerna (2000)

cxxviii Daraganova, G. (2013). Is it ok to be away? School attendance in the primary school years. In G. Daraganova, B. Maguire, J. Kaspar, & B. Edwards (Eds.), The longitudinal study of Australian children: Annual statistical report 2012 (pp. 59–76). Canberra, ACT: Australian Institute of Family Studies.; Hanly, M., Edwards, B., Goldfeld, S., Craven, R. G., Mooney, J., Jorm, L., & Falster, K. (2019). School starting age and child development in a state-wide, population- level cohort of children in their first year of school in New South Wales, Australia. *Early Childhood Research Quarterly, 48*, 325–340.

cxxix Larsen, S. A., Little, C. W., & Coventry, W. L. (2020). Exploring the associations between delayed school entry and achievement in primary and secondary school. *Child Development.*

cxxx Lubotsky, D., & Kaestner, R. (2016). DoSkills Beget Skills'? Evidence on the effect of kindergarten entrance age on the evolution of cognitive and non-cognitive skill gaps in childhood. *Economics of Education Review, 53*, 194-206.

cxxxi Black, Devereux, and Salvanes (2011).

cxxxii Cook, P. J., & Kang, S. (2016). Birthdays, schooling, and crime: Regression-discontinuity analysis of school performance, delinquency, dropout, and crime initiation. *American Economic Journal: Applied Economics, 8* (1), 33-57.

cxxxiii Bai, J. J., Ma, L., Mullally, K. A., & Solomon, D. H. (2019). What a difference a (birth) month makes: The relative age effect and fund manager performance. *Journal of Financial Economics, 132*(1), 200-221.

cxxxiv Fredriksson, Peter, & Ockert, B. (2006). Is early learning really more productive? The effect of school starting age on school and labor market performance. IZAWorking Paper No. 2006:12, Bonn, Germany.

cxxxv Black, S. E., Devereux, P. J., & Salvanes, K. G. (2008). Staying in the classroom and out of the maternity ward? The effect of compulsory schooling laws on teenage births. *The Economic Journal, 118* (530), 1025-1054.

cxxxvi Breining, S., Doyle, J., Figlio, D. N., Karbownik, K., & Roth, J. (2020). Birth order and delinquency: Evidence from Denmark and Florida. *Journal of Labor Economics, 38*(1), 95-142.

cxxxvii Potter, D., & Morris, D. S. (2017). Family and schooling experiences in racial/ethnic academic achievement gaps: A cumulative perspective. *Sociological Perspectives, 60* (1), 132-167.

cxxxviii Norbury, C. F., Gooch, D., Baird, G., Charman, T., Simonoff, E., & Pickles, A. (2016). Younger children experience lower levels of language competence and academic progress in the first year of school: evidence from a population study. *Journal of Child Psychology and Psychiatry, 57* (1), 65-73.

cxxxix See p. 642 of Elder and Lubotsky (2009).

cxl See p. 645 of Elder and Lubotsky (2009).

cxli Peña, P. A. (2017). Creating winners and losers: Date of birth, relative age in school, and outcomes in childhood and adulthood. *Economics of Education Review, 56*, 152-176.

cxlii E.g., Holmes (1989).

cxliii Fruehwirth, J. C., Navarro, S., & Takahashi, Y. (2016). How the timing of grade retention affects outcomes: Identification and estimation of time-varying treatment effects. *Journal of Labor Economics, 34*(4), 979-1021.

cxliv Dhuey, E., Figlio, D., Karbownik, K., & Roth, J. (2019). School starting age and cognitive development. *Journal of Policy Analysis and Management, 38*, 538-578.

cxlv Christopher, C., & Farran, D. (2020). Academic gains in kindergarten related to eight classroom practices. *Early Childhood Research Quarterly, 53*, 638-649.

cxlvi Allen, J., & Barnsley, R. (1993). Streams and tiers: The interaction of ability, maturity, and training in systems with age-dependent recursive selection. *The Journal of Human Resources, 28*(3), 649-659.

cxlvii Glamser, F. D., & Vincent, J. (2004). The Relative Age Effect Among Elite American Youth Soccer Players. *Journal of sport Behavior, 27*(1).

cxlviii Musch, J., & Grondin, S. (2001). Unequal competition as an impediment to personal development: A review of the relative age effect in sport. *Developmental review, 21*(2), 147-167.

cxlix Delorme, N., Boiché, J., & Raspaud, M. (2009). The relative age effect in elite sport: the French case. *Research quarterly for exercise and sport, 80*(2), 336-344.

cl Furley, P., & Memmert, D. (2016). Coaches' implicit associations between size and giftedness: implications for the relative age effect. *Journal of Sports Sciences, 34*(5), 459-466.

cli Doyle, J. R., & Bottomley, P. A. (2018). Relative age effect in elite soccer: More early-born players, but no better valued, and no paragon clubs or countries. *PloS one, 13*(2), e0192209.

clii Doyle, J. R., Bottomley, P. A., & Angell, R. (2017). Tails of the Travelling Gaussian model and the relative age effect: Tales of age discrimination and wasted talent. *PloS one, 12*(4), e0176206.

cliii See http://www.charactercenter.com/Insight/InsightMarch2.htm; www.ncaa.org/research/, www.dailynebraskan.com; https://theineffablepastime.wordpress.com/2017/05/03/my-child-the-next-great-american-sports-star/

cliv Howe, M. J. (2001). *Genius explained.* Cambridge University Press.

clv Ericsson, K. A., Krampe, R. T., & Tesch-Römer, C. (1993). The role of deliberate practice in the acquisition of expert performance. *Psychological Review, 100*(3), 363.

clvi See p. 195 of Howe (2001).

clvii Sloboda, J. A., Davidson, J. W., Howe, M. J., & Moore, D. G. (1996). The role of practice in the development of performing musicians. *British Journal of Psychology, 87*(2), 287-309.

clviii See p. 205 of Howe (2001).

clix Hyson, M. (2008). *Enthusiastic and engaged learners: Approaches to learning in the early childhood classroom.* New York: Teachers College Press.

clx Guthrie, J. T., Wigfield, A., & VonSecker, C. (2000). Effects of integrated instruction on motivation and strategy use in reading. *Journal of Educational Psychology, 92*(2), 331.

clxi Lareau, A. (2011). *Unequal childhoods: Class, race, and family life.* Berkley: University of California Press.

clxii Bourdieu, P. (1973). *Cultural reproduction and social reproduction.* London: Tavistock.

clxiii Bourdieu, P. (1973).

clxiv Lareau, A. (2000). *Home advantage: Social class and parental intervention in elementary education.* New York: Rowman & Littlefield Publishers.: Lareau (2011).

clxv Bassok et al. (2016).

Chapter 5

clxvi Goldstein, L. S. (2007). Beyond the DAP versus standards dilemma: Examining the unforgiving complexity of kindergarten teaching in the United States. *Early Childhood Research Quarterly, 22*(1), 39-54.

clxvii Brown, C. P., Barry, D. P., Ku, D. H., & Englehardt, J. (2020). How Education Stakeholders Made Sense of the Types of Learning Experiences Children are and Should be Having in Kindergarten and Why. *Early Education and Development,* 1-32.

clxviii Dr. Jennifer Adair, Dr. Joanna Englehardt, and Natalie Weber.

clxix Adair, J. K., Colgrove, K. S. S., & McManus, M. E. (2018). Troubling messages: Agency and learning in the early schooling experiences of children of Latinx immigrants. *Teachers College Record, 120,* 1-40.; Tobin, J., Hseuh, Y., & Karasawa, M. (2009). *Preschool in three cultures Revisited China,*

Japan, and the United States. Chicago: The University of Chicago Press.

clxx In Texas, students are expected to recite the pledge of allegiance to the US flag and the Texas pledge (see https://texas.public.law/statutes/tex._educ._code_section_25.082)

clxxi Brown, C. P. (2021).

clxxii Brown and Weber (2016a).

clxxiii See p. 91 of Wilson, J. M. (2018). *The human side of changing education: How to lead change with clarity, conviction, and courage.* Corwin Press.

clxxiv Brown, C. P., Weber, N. B. (2016b). Working with practicing teachers in a high-stakes teaching context to rethink their pedagogical practices with children of diverse backgrounds. *Action in Teacher Education, 38* (3), 259-277.

clxxv See p. 462 of Hatch (2002).

clxxvi Powell, K. S. (1969). Kindergarten is not sitting at a desk with a workbook and sharpened pencil. In D. K. Osborn (Ed.), *Kindergarten: Who? What? Where?* (pp. 34-35). Athens, GA: Southern Association on Children Under Six.

clxxvii Lynch, M. (2015). More play please: The perspectives of kindergarten teachers on play in the classroom. *American Journal of Play, 7*, 347–370.

clxxviii See p. 308 of Minicozzi, L. L. (2016). The garden is thorny: Teaching kindergarten in the age of accountability. *Global Studies of Childhood, 6*, 299-310.

clxxix Ball, S. (2003). The teacher's soul and the terrors of performativity. *Journal of Education Policy, 18* (2), 215–228.; Lewis, S., & Holloway, J. (2019). Datafying the teaching 'profession': Remaking the professional teacher in the image of data. *Cambridge Journal of Education, 49*(1), 35-51.

clxxx See p. 17 of Weisenfeld, G. G., Garver, K., & Hodges, K. (2020): Federal and state efforts in the

implementation of kindergarten entry assessments (2011-2018). *Early Education and Development.* DOI: 10.1080/10409289.2020.1720481

clxxxi Christopher and Farran (2020).

clxxxii Sonnenschein, S., Stapleton, L. M., & Benson, A. (2010). The relation between the type and amount of instruction and growth in children's reading competencies. *American Educational Research Journal, 47* (2), 358–389.

clxxxiii Durden, T., & Dangel, J. (2008). Teacher-involved conversations with young children during small group activity. *Early Years, 28,* 251–266.; Siekkinen, M., Pakarinen, E., Lerkkanen, M., Poikkeus, A., Salminen, J., Poskiparta, E., . . . & Nurmi, J. (2013). Social competence among 6-year-old children and classroom instructional support and teacher stress. *Early Education and Development, 24* (6), 877–897.

clxxxiv Hyson (2008).

clxxxv Wilson (2018).

Chapter 6

clxxxvi Willingham, D. T. (2009). *Why don't students like school?: A cognitive scientist answers questions about how the mind works and what it means for the classroom.* New Yor: John Wiley & Sons.

clxxxvii Brown, Feger, & Mowry (2018).

clxxxviii Anderson, P. M., Butcher, K. F., Hoynes, H. W., & Whitmore Schanzenbach, D. (2016). Beyond income: what else predicts very low food security among children?. *Southern Economic Journal, 82*(4), 1078-1105.; Dee, T. S., & Jacob, B. (2011). The impact of No Child Left Behind on student achievement. *Journal of Policy Analysis and management, 30*(3), 418-446.

clxxxix Saavedra, C. M., & Marx, S. (2016). Schooling as taming wild tongues and bodies. *Global Studies of Childhood, 6*(1), 42-52.

cxc Castelli, D. M., Hillman, C. H., Buck, S. M., & Erwin, H. E. (2007). Physical fitness and academic achievement in third-and fifth-grade students. *Journal of Sport and Exercise Psychology, 29*(2), 239-252.; Mavilidi, M. F., Okely, A. D., Chandler, P., Cliff, D. P., & Paas, F. (2015). Effects of integrated physical exercises and gestures on preschool children's foreign language vocabulary learning. *Educational Psychology Review, 27*(3), 413-426.

cxci Chang, Y. K., Tsai, Y. J., Chen, T. T., & Hung, T. M. (2013). The impacts of coordinative exercise on executive function in kindergarten children: an ERP study. *Experimental Brain Research, 225*(2), 187-196.

cxcii Graham, G., Hale, S. A., & Parker, M. (2009). *Children moving: a reflective approach to teaching physical education (8th ed).* New York: McGraw-Hill.

cxciii Willinghan (2009).

cxciv Freire, P. (2006) [1970]. The banking model of education. In E. F. Provenzo (ed.), *Critical issues in education: An anthology of readings* (pp. 105-117). Thousand Oaks, CA: SAGE.

cxcv Willingham (2009).

cxcvi National Research Council, Donovan, S., & Bransford, J. (2005). *How students learn.* Washington, DC: National Academies Press.; Willingham (2009).

cxcvii Diamond, A. (2013). Executive functions. *Annual Review of Psychology, 64,* 135-168.

cxcviii Miyake, A., Friedman, N. P., Emerson, M. J., Witzki, A. H., Howerter, A., & Wager, T. D. (2000). The unity and diversity of executive functions and their contributions to complex "frontal lobe" tasks: A latent variable analysis. *Cognitive psychology, 41*(1), 49-100.

cxcix Blair, C., & Razza, R. P. (2007). Relating effortful control, executive function, and false belief understanding to emerging math and literacy ability in kindergarten. *Child Development, 78* (2), 647-663.; Brock, L. L., Rimm-Kaufman, S. E., Nathanson, L., & Grimm, K. J. (2009). The contributions of 'hot'and 'cool'executive function to children's academic achievement, learning-related behaviors, and engagement in kindergarten. *Early Childhood Research Quarterly, 24* (3), 337-349.

cc Brown, Feger, and Mowry (2018).

cci Johnston, P. H. (2012). *Opening minds: Using language to change lives.* Portland, ME: Stenhouse Publishers.

ccii Dweck, C. S. (2006). *Mindset: The new psychology of success.* New York: Random House.

cciii Johnston, P. H. (2004). *Choice words: How our language affects children's learning.* Stenhouse Publishers.; Johnston (2012).

cciv See p. 2 of Johnston (2012).

ccv See p. 12 of Johnston (2012).

ccvi Walt Disney Animation Studios ; directed by Chris Buck, Jennifer Lee ; produced by Peter Del Vecho ; screenplay by Jennifer Lee ; story by Chris Buck, Jennifer Lee, Shane Morris. (2013). *Frozen*. Burbank, Calif. :Walt Disney Pictures.

ccvii Here's a link to Dweck's TED Talk on a growth mindset: https://www.ted.com/talks/carol_dweck_the_power_of_believing_th at_you_can_improve

ccviii Here's a link to Duckworth's TED Talk on grit: https://www.ted.com/talks/angela_lee_duckworth_grit_the_power_o f_passion_and_perseverance/transcript?language=en

ccix Ryan, R. M., & Deci, E. L. (2000). Intrinsic and extrinsic motivations: Classic definitions and new directions. *Contemporary educational psychology, 25*(1), 54-67.

ccx Adair, J. K. (2014). Agency and expanding capabilities in early grade classrooms: What it could mean for young children. *Harvard Educational Review, 84,* 217-241.; Kundu, A. (2020). *The power of student agency: Looking beyond grit to close the opportunity gap.* New York: Teachers College Press.

ccxi See p. 25 of Street, B.V. (1993). Culture is a verb. In D. Graddol, L. Thompson, & M. Byram (Eds), *Language and Culture* (pp. 23-43). London: BAAL/ Multilingual Matters.

ccxii See p. 6 of Goodwin, A. L., Cheruvu, R., & Genishi, C. (2008). Responding to multiple diversities in early childhood education. In C. Genishi & A. L. Goodwin (Eds.), *Diversities in early childhood education: Rethinking and doing* (pp. 3-10). New York: Routledge.

ccxiii Brown et al. (2018).

ccxiv See p. 52 of Rogoff, B. (2003). *The cultural nature of human development.* Oxford: Oxford University Press.

ccxv Rogoff (2003).

ccxvi Heath, S. B. (1983). *Ways with words: Language, life and work in communities and classrooms.* Cambridge: Cambridge University Press.

ccxvii See p. 10 of Brown and Lan (2015).

ccxviii Corsaro, W. A. (2017). *The sociology of childhood.* Thousand Oaks, CA: SAGE.

ccxix Rogoff (2003).

ccxx Kundu (2020).

ccxxi See Valencia (1997).

ccxxii Nxumalo, F., & Brown, C. P. (2019). *Disrupting and countering deficits in early childhood education.* New York: Routledge.

ccxxiii If you're curious how the typical development of children is discussed, I would suggest looking at these 2 articles that outline what 4 and 5 years-old are typically able to do: For 4 year-olds: https://www.nytimes.com/2020/04/18/parenting/milestones/4-year-old.html and for 5 year-olds: https://www.nytimes.com/2020/04/18/parenting/milestones/5-year-old.html?searchResultPosition=9

ccxxiv Katz, L. G., Chard, S. C.(2000). *Engaging children's minds: The project approach.* Santa Barbara, CA: Greenwood Publishing Group.

ccxxv Brown et al. (2018).

ccxxvi Katz and Chard (2000).

ccxxvii Vygotsky (1978).

ccxxviii Hatch (2019).

ccxxix Gopnik, A. (2012). Scientific thinking in young children: Theoretical advances, empirical research, and policy implications. *Science, 337*(6102), 1623-1627.

ccxxx Gopnik, A., Meltzoff, A. N., & Kuhl, P. K. (2000). *The scientist in the crib: What early learning tells us about the mind.* New York: William Morrow Paperbacks.

ccxxxi Hyson (2008).

ccxxxii See p. 9 of Brown et al., 2018.

Chapter 7

ccxxxiii UC-Chino has developed this summary, but it may not be up to date:
https://www.chino.k12.ca.us/site/handlers/filedownload.ashx?modul
einstanceid=28620&dataid=54444&FileName=0%20ccss%20ela%20k
inder%20standards.pdf

ccxxxiv Many of the ideas I write about in this chapter comes from my other book *RIGOROUS DAP in the early years: From theory to practice* (2018): St. Paul, MN: Redleaf Press. I wrote that book with Beth S. Feger (the 'redo' friend) and Brian N. Mowry. They've given me permission to draw from these ideas in this book.

ccxxxv Schickedanz, J. A. (1999). *Much more than the ABCs: The early stages of reading and writing.* Washington, DC: NAEYC.

ccxxxvi Adams, M. J., Forman, B., Lundberg, I., & Beeler, T. (2003). *Phonemic awareness in young children.* Baltimore: Paul H. Brookes Publishing.

ccxxxvii Baroody, A. J., & Li, X. (2009). Mathematics instruction that makes sense for 2 to 5 year olds. *Development and Education: Research Reviews from Young Children,* 119-135.

ccxxxviii National Research Council. (2012). *A framework for K-12 science education: Practices, crosscutting concepts, and core ideas.* Washington, DC: National Academies Press.

ccxxxix National Research Council (2012).

ccxl National Science Teachers Association. (2014). NSTA position statement: Early childhood science education. *Science and Children,* 51(7), 10-12.

ccxli Gopnik (2012).

ccxlii National Council for the Social Studies. (2010). *National curriculum standards for social studies: A framework for teaching, learning, and assessment.* Washington, DC: Author.

ccxliii Walker, T. D. (2015). The joyful, illiterate kindergartners of Finland. *The Atlantic,* 1.